The Seduction Blueprint: Confidence, Attraction, and Success with Women

Copyright © 2025 by Chase M. Klein

All rights reserved.

Permission to reproduce or transmit in any form or by any means, electronic or mechanical, including photocopying, photographic and recording audio or video, or by any information storage and retrieval system, must be obtained in writing from the author.

The Seduction Blueprint: Confidence, Attraction, and Success with Women is a registered trademark of Chase M. Klein.

First printing March 2025

Paperback ISBN: 9798314955833

Printed in the U.S.A.

The Seduction Blueprint

Confidence, Attraction, and Success with Women

Chase M. Klein

Table of Contents

Introduction   v

Chapter 1

The Core Principle of Attraction – Confidence and Self-Assurance   1

Chapter 2

How to Rewire Your Mind for Success with Women   7

Chapter 3

Mastering Social Presence and Emotional Intelligence   13

Chapter 4

Developing a High-Value Mindset   19

Chapter 5

Overcoming Fear of Rejection and Setbacks   25

Chapter 6

First Impressions – Making a Lasting Impact   31

Chapter 7

The Art of Conversation – Building Instant Chemistry   37

Chapter 8

Understanding Female Psychology and Attraction Triggers   45

Chapter 9
  Where to Meet Women – High-Yield Environments
  for Connection   53
Chapter 10
  How to Flirt and Create Romantic Tension   61
Chapter 11
  How to Navigate Group Dynamics and Social
  Proof   69
Chapter 12
  The Art of Getting Her Number and Following Up   77
Chapter 13
  Planning and Leading Memorable Dates   85
Chapter 14
  Building Emotional and Physical Connection   93
Chapter 15
  Handling Rejection and Keeping High Standards   101
Chapter 16
  Turning a Date into a Meaningful Relationship
  (or Casual Encounter)   109
Chapter 17
  The Long-Term Game – Keeping Her Interested
  and Avoiding Complacency   115

Chapter 18

   Mastering the Breakup – When to Walk Away and
   How to Move On   121

Chapter 19

   The Mindset of a Man Who Never Struggles with
   Women   127

Chapter 20

   Final Thoughts – Becoming the Man You Were
   Meant to Be   133

Appendix   139

About the Author   149

Introduction

Unlocking the Power of Confidence, Attraction, and Success with Women

Let's get one thing straight right away—**attraction is not about tricks, gimmicks, or manipulation.** If you've come here hoping for a magic pickup line that'll make women fall into your lap, let me save you some time: that's not how this works.

But if you're looking for something real—something that **gives you the power to naturally attract women without feeling fake, nervous, or second-guessing yourself**—then keep reading.

Because that's exactly what this book is about.

I've seen too many men struggle unnecessarily. Good men. Smart, hardworking guys who are **successful in other areas of life but feel completely lost when it comes to women.** They feel like they're **stuck in the "friend zone," constantly chasing women who show no interest, or fumbling when the moment comes to take things to the next level.**

Sound familiar?

Here's the good news: attraction isn't some mystical force that only "lucky" guys understand. It's not something you're either born with or doomed to live without. **Attraction is a skill—one that you can learn, develop, and master.**

And it all starts with **you**.

Why This Book Exists

There are a million "dating guides" out there, most of them promising quick-fix techniques. Some focus on **memorizing pickup lines**, others on **manipulative persuasion tactics**, and a few dive into **the science of attraction without any practical application**.

But **this book is different**.

Instead of selling you a fantasy, I'm going to show you how to **actually become the kind of man that women are naturally drawn to.**

I'm talking about real confidence—not fake bravado. Genuine connection—not rehearsed scripts. Authentic attraction—not manipulation.

Because let's be honest—**women aren't stupid.** They can smell insecurity and desperation a mile away. And **if you're trying too hard to impress them, you've already lost.**

What we're going to do in this book is **fundamentally shift the way you think about attraction** so that you can approach women with confidence, certainty, and ease.

By the time you're done reading, you won't need gimmicks. You won't need to memorize lines. **You'll just be you—at your best.**

What You'll Learn Inside

This book is built in four parts, each designed to take you **from where you are now to where you want to be.**

- **Part One: The Mindset of Attraction** – Before you can succeed with women, you have to **master yourself.** We'll dive into confidence, self-assurance, and overcoming fear.

- **Part Two: Meeting and Connecting with Women** – You'll learn **how to start conversations, create chemistry, and build attraction effortlessly.**

- **Part Three: The Dating Process** – From getting her number to planning an unforgettable date, you'll learn how to **keep the connection growing.**

- **Part Four: Advanced Attraction Techniques** – We'll explore **body language, storytelling, and long-term attraction strategies** that make you stand out.

But here's the real secret: **this book isn't just about women—it's about you.**

If you truly apply what you learn here, you won't just become better at dating. **You'll become a stronger, more confident man in every area of your life.**

Your career, your friendships, your self-worth—it's all connected.

How to Get the Most Out of This Book

1. **Forget everything you think you know about dating.** If you've been struggling, it means your current approach isn't working. Time to reset.
2. **Do the work.** This isn't just a book to read—it's a book to apply. There will be exercises, mindset shifts, and real-world challenges. **The more you put in, the more you'll get out.**
3. **Trust the process.** Change doesn't happen overnight, but if you stick with it, you'll be amazed at how quickly things start to shift.

And one last thing…

This book isn't here to turn you into someone you're not.

It's here to bring out the best version of who you already are.

Let's get started.

Chapter 1

The Core Principle of Attraction – Confidence and Self-Assurance

The Truth About Attraction

Let's cut through the noise right away: **confidence is the single most attractive trait a man can have.** Not money, not looks, not clever pickup lines—confidence.

And I don't mean the fake, overcompensating kind of confidence where a guy tries to "peacock" his way into a woman's attention. I'm talking about **real, unshakable self-assurance**—the kind that makes people stop and pay attention when you walk into a room.

Here's the thing: women don't just like confidence. **They crave it.** It's wired into human psychology.

Confidence signals **strength, competence, and certainty**—qualities that naturally make someone a leader, a protector, and someone worth investing in.

And the best part? **Confidence isn't something you're born with. It's something you build.**

Why Most Guys Get This Wrong

Most men struggle with attraction because they focus on **tactics** instead of **identity**.

They want the perfect opening line.

They want a formula that guarantees results.

They want a shortcut.

But here's the brutal truth: **you can have all the best tactics in the world, but if you lack confidence, none of them will work.**

Women pick up on insecurity instantly. **It shows in your body language, the way you speak, and the way you react when things don't go your way.**

And nothing kills attraction faster than a man who **seeks validation instead of standing in his own power.**

What Real Confidence Looks Like

Here's a **simple but powerful mindset shift**: confidence **is not about what you say or do—it's about how you feel about yourself.**

A truly confident man doesn't need approval from women. **He knows his own value, regardless of how anyone else reacts.**

He doesn't flinch when a woman tests him. He doesn't change his personality to fit what he thinks she wants.

He doesn't put women on a pedestal.

Instead, he **moves through the world without apology.**

He takes up space.

He speaks with certainty.

He knows that if one woman isn't interested, **another one will be.**

And this is what makes him magnetic.

How to Build Unshakable Confidence

If confidence is a skill, how do you build it?

Here's where we get into the **practical steps.**

1. Fix Your Posture and Body Language

Before you say a word, **your body already communicates who you are.**

- **Stand up straight.** Shoulders back, chest open.
- **Slow down your movements.** Rushed, jerky movements signal nervousness.
- **Make strong eye contact.** Not in a creepy way—just enough to show presence.

Try this next time you enter a room: **walk in like you belong there.** Even if you don't feel it at first, your body will train your mind to follow.

2. Stop Seeking Approval

Most guys subconsciously look for permission when talking to women. **They over-explain, justify themselves, or wait for validation before making a move.**

Confident men? **They act as if they already belong.**

- If you want to ask her out, **ask.**
- If you want to kiss her, **go for it when the moment is right.**
- If you have an opinion, **state it without hesitation.**

Women respect men who **own their decisions.**

3. Accept Rejection Without Losing Power

Here's a mindset shift that will **change your life:**

Rejection is not about you.

Most of the time, it's about **her mood, her past experiences, or her personal preferences**—things you **can't control.**

Confident men **don't internalize rejection.** They shrug it off and move forward.

- She's not interested? **Cool. Next.**
- She's playing games? **Not worth your time.**
- She ghosts you? **Her loss.**

When you stop fearing rejection, you become **unstoppable.**

4. Develop a Life That Excites You

Confidence isn't just about women—it's about **how you live your life.**

If you have nothing going for you outside of chasing women, **they will sense it.**

A man who has **a mission, goals, and passions** naturally becomes attractive.
- Find a hobby you love.
- Build a career that excites you.
- Surround yourself with people who push you to grow.

When your life is already amazing, women **want to be part of it.**

The Takeaway

Confidence is **not** about memorizing tricks or forcing yourself to act a certain way. It's about:
- **Owning who you are**
- **Not seeking approval**
- **Moving through the world with certainty**

When you **stop chasing validation** and start **living with self-assurance**, attraction happens naturally.

No gimmicks. No games. **Just you—at your best.**

Chapter 2

How to Rewire Your Mind for Success with Women

Why Mindset is Everything

Before we get into techniques, approaches, and strategies, let's address the **real reason most guys struggle with women**—their mindset.

Because the truth is, **your results with women are a direct reflection of what you believe about yourself, attraction, and dating.**

If you believe:

- "I'm not good enough."
- "Women only want rich, good-looking guys."
- "I always get rejected."
- "I'm just unlucky with women."

...then that's exactly what you'll experience.

Your brain is **a powerful filter.** It takes the beliefs you hold as truth and then looks for proof in the real world to confirm them. This is called **confirmation bias.**

So if you think women don't like you, your brain will **ignore all the positive signals** and **only focus on rejection.**

If you believe you're unattractive, you'll **project insecurity** and sabotage yourself before you even get started.

Here's the good news: **your beliefs are not facts.**

They are **mental programs you've picked up over time.**

And just like any program, they can be **rewritten.**

Reprogramming Your Beliefs About Women and Attraction

If you want **different results**, you need to start by **changing the way you think.**

And the fastest way to do that is by **challenging and replacing limiting beliefs.**

Let's break it down step by step:

1. Identify the Limiting Beliefs Holding You Back

The first step in changing your mindset is recognizing **what's keeping you stuck.**

Think about the last time you saw a beautiful woman you wanted to talk to but didn't.

What thoughts ran through your head?

- "She's probably not interested in me."
- "I don't want to embarrass myself."
- "She's out of my league."
- "I'll just get rejected."

Now, ask yourself: **Are these thoughts facts or assumptions?**

Most of the time, they're just **stories you've been telling yourself.** And these stories have **zero basis in reality.**

A woman being attractive **doesn't mean she's uninterested.**

Rejection **doesn't mean failure**—it means she's not the right fit.

Confidence **isn't about being fearless—it's about taking action despite fear.**

The key here is to **question everything you assume about attraction.** Because when you **see the lie**, you can replace it with the truth.

2. Install New, Powerful Beliefs

Once you've identified the **bullshit stories** that have been running your dating life, it's time to **replace them with beliefs that actually serve you.**

Here are some powerful mindset shifts to adopt:

- **Old Belief:** "Women don't like guys like me."
  New Belief: "Women love confident, self-assured men, and I'm becoming one."

- **Old Belief:** "I have to be rich and good-looking to attract women."
- **New Belief:** "Attraction is about personality, energy, and confidence—not just money or looks."
- **Old Belief:** "If I get rejected, it means I'm not good enough."
- **New Belief:** "Rejection is just redirection to someone better suited for me."

These aren't just **positive affirmations**—they're **fundamental shifts in the way you see yourself and the world.**

3. Take Small, Daily Actions That Reinforce Your New Beliefs

Your brain **learns best through experience.** So if you want to **truly internalize these new beliefs,** you need to **prove them to yourself** with small actions every day.

Here's how:

- **Approach one woman a day** just to say hello. No expectations, just practice.
- **Stand up straighter, make eye contact, and own your space** wherever you go.
- **Start conversations with strangers**—not just women, but people in general.

Every time you **take action**, you collect **proof** that you are the kind of man who is **capable, confident, and attractive.**

And the more proof you collect, the stronger your **new identity** becomes.

The Fastest Way to Develop an Unstoppable Mindset

If you want to truly rewire your brain for success with women, here's a simple but **powerful exercise** you should do **every single morning**:

The Identity Reprogramming Exercise

1. **Stand in front of a mirror.** Look yourself in the eyes.
2. **Say out loud:**
   - "I am a confident man who attracts women effortlessly."
   - "I create connections wherever I go."
   - "I am completely comfortable around beautiful women."
3. **Visualize yourself walking into a room with total confidence.** See yourself relaxed, smiling, and in control.
4. **Carry this energy into your day.**

This might feel weird at first—but that's because you're **breaking years of mental programming.**

Stick with it. You'll be amazed at how quickly your mindset shifts.

The Takeaway

Attraction starts in your mind. **If you believe you're not good enough, no amount of dating advice will help you.**

But if you train yourself to **think like a confident man, you will naturally become one.**

Rewire your beliefs.

Take small, daily actions.

Step into the identity of the man you want to be.

Do this consistently, and women **will start noticing you in a way they never have before.**

Chapter 3

Mastering Social Presence and Emotional Intelligence

Why Social Presence is the Ultimate Attraction Booster

Ever notice how some men **command attention the second they walk into a room**—without even saying a word?

That's **social presence** in action.

Social presence is **the energy you bring into any interaction**. It's how people **perceive you, feel about you, and respond to you** before you even open your mouth.

Women are **highly attuned to this.** They can instantly sense whether a man is:

✓ **Confident and self-assured**

✓ **Anxious and unsure**

✓ **Trying too hard to impress**

And here's the best part: **social presence is something you can develop.**

When you master it, you'll **never have to chase women again—because they will be drawn to you.**

The Secret to Magnetic Presence: Being Fully Present

Most men kill their own social presence without realizing it.

They do this by **living in their heads**—constantly overthinking, analyzing, and second-guessing themselves.

- "What should I say next?"
- "Is she losing interest?"
- "What if I mess this up?"

The moment you **start thinking instead of being present, you lose attraction.**

Women don't want a man who's trapped in his own thoughts. They want a man who is **grounded, aware, and engaged in the moment.**

How to Become Fully Present in Conversations

The next time you're talking to a woman (or anyone, really), try this:

1. **Focus on your breathing.** Feel the air going in and out of your lungs. This keeps you grounded.
2. **Slow down your speech and movements.** Confidence is relaxed, not rushed.

3. **Listen fully before responding.** Don't just wait for your turn to talk—really absorb what she's saying.
4. **Make intentional eye contact.** Not staring—just enough to show that you're engaged and confident.

Presence isn't about **what you say**—it's about how you **make people feel when they're around you.**

Emotional Intelligence: The Key to Deep Connection

If social presence gets you **noticed**, emotional intelligence keeps a woman **interested.**

Emotional intelligence (EQ) is your ability to:

- **Read social cues** and understand what people are feeling
- **Adjust your approach** based on the energy of the conversation
- **Make people feel comfortable and understood**

And here's the good news: **you don't have to be born with it. You can develop it.**

The 3 Pillars of Emotional Intelligence for Attraction

1. Read Her Nonverbal Cues

Most of what women communicate isn't in their words—it's in their **body language, tone, and micro-expressions.**

Pay attention to things like:

✓ **Does she lean in or pull away when you talk?**
✓ **Is her voice engaged and playful, or flat and distant?**
✓ **Is she mirroring your energy and movements?**

These signals tell you **if she's interested, bored, or testing you.**

And the more you **tune in**, the easier it becomes to respond in a way that deepens attraction.

2. Control Your Emotional State

Most men lose women's interest because they **react emotionally instead of leading the interaction.**

- She teases them → They get defensive.
- She takes her time texting back → They get needy.
- She plays hard to get → They get frustrated.

A high-value man? **He stays cool no matter what.**

How to develop this? **Pause before reacting.**

If something triggers you, take a deep breath and ask yourself:

- "Is this actually a big deal, or am I just reacting emotionally?"
- "How would a confident, high-status man handle this?"

Women are **attracted to emotional strength.** The more control you have over your emotions, the more magnetic you become.

3. Make Her Feel Understood

Women don't just want a man who talks **about himself—** they want a man who can **connect with them emotionally.**

One of the fastest ways to build attraction is to **make her feel like you truly "get" her.**

Here's how:

- **Use reflective listening.** Instead of just waiting to talk, repeat key points she says:
    - **Her:** "I love traveling, but I never have time."
    - **You:** "Sounds like you crave adventure but get stuck in your routine."
- **Ask deeper questions.** Instead of "What do you do for work?" try "What do you love most about what you do?"
- **Share relatable experiences.** If she talks about a struggle, **don't just offer solutions—relate to her experience.**

When a woman feels truly understood, **she naturally starts feeling more attracted to you.**

Putting It All Together: The Charisma Formula

If you combine **social presence** with **emotional intelligence**, you become **naturally charismatic.**

And charisma is what makes women **gravitate toward you.**

Here's the simple **Charisma Formula** to follow in every interaction:

1. **Stay present.** Get out of your head and into the moment.

2. **Read her energy.** Notice how she's responding to you.

3. **Stay emotionally grounded.** Don't get thrown off by small tests or challenges.

4. **Make her feel understood.** Connect on an emotional level, not just a logical one.

The more you practice this, the **easier and more natural attraction becomes.**

The Takeaway

Attraction isn't just about what you say—it's about **who you are when you say it.**

When you develop **strong social presence** and **high emotional intelligence**, you:

✓ **Command attention effortlessly**

✓ **Create instant chemistry**

✓ **Make women feel drawn to you without trying too hard**

And the best part?

These skills don't just make you better with women. **They make you more powerful in every area of life.**

Master this, and you **become the kind of man who naturally stands out—wherever you go.**

Chapter 4

Developing a High-Value Mindset

What It Means to Be a High-Value Man

Let's get one thing straight: **Women don't chase "nice guys." They chase high-value men.**

And no, a high-value man isn't just someone who's rich, famous, or looks like a movie star.

A **high-value man** is a guy who:

✓ Knows his worth and never settles for less

✓ Prioritizes his own growth and success

✓ Lives with purpose and confidence

✓ Naturally attracts people because he's on a mission

He doesn't need to **convince a woman to like him**—he's too focused on building an amazing life, and women **want to be part of it.**

The mistake most men make? **They make women the center of their world.**

High-value men? **They make their world so incredible that women want to join it.**

Why Most Men Get Stuck in the Low-Value Mindset

Most guys don't struggle with women because they're "not good enough."

They struggle because they **think and act in ways that lower their own value.**

Here are **three signs you're stuck in a low-value mindset:**

1. You Seek Validation Instead of Respect

Low-value men **chase approval** from women.

They try too hard to impress.

They put women on a pedestal.

They get anxious when a woman isn't giving them attention.

High-value men? **They never beg for validation.**

They know that their worth isn't determined by whether or not a woman likes them.

They demand respect instead of chasing approval.

Mindset Shift: You don't need validation from women—you need to validate yourself.

2. You Put Women Above Your Purpose

Low-value men **make women their mission.**

They drop their hobbies, their goals, and their own growth **just to impress a woman.**

High-value men? **They put their purpose first.**

Women are a great addition to their life—but **they are not the center of it.**

Mindset Shift: Make your life so exciting that women want to be part of it.

3. You Operate from Scarcity Instead of Abundance

Low-value men act like every woman they meet is their **last shot at happiness.**

- They get clingy.
- They fear rejection.
- They stay in bad relationships because they think they "won't find anyone else."

High-value men operate from **abundance.**

- They know there are **plenty of incredible women** out there.
- They **walk away from bad situations** without hesitation.
- They know that **their value attracts the right people—without forcing anything.**

Mindset Shift: You don't chase women—you attract them by being the best version of yourself.

The 3 Core Beliefs of a High-Value Man

If you want to be a **man that women respect, admire, and desire**, you need to start thinking like one.

Here's how:

1. "I Am the Prize"

A high-value man **sees himself as the catch.**

He doesn't think, **"I hope she likes me."**

He thinks, **"Let's see if she's good enough for me."**

This isn't arrogance—it's **self-respect.**

How to Implement This:

- The next time you talk to a woman, **shift your mindset.** Instead of trying to win her over, **assess if she's actually right for you.**
- **Stop prioritizing women who don't prioritize you.** If she's playing games, **walk away.**

2. "My Purpose Comes First"

A high-value man is **obsessed with his mission.**

- He has **goals bigger than just dating.**
- He's focused on **building his career, health, and personal growth.**
- He sees women as **a great addition to his life—not the main event.**

How to Implement This:

- Get **clear on your mission**—What are you building? What excites you?
- Invest in yourself **every day**—Read, hit the gym, grow your skills.
- **Never compromise your purpose** for a woman.

3. "I Have Standards"

A high-value man **doesn't accept just any woman into his life.**

- He doesn't tolerate **bad behavior or disrespect.**
- He's willing to **walk away from toxic situations.**
- He values **quality over quantity.**

How to Implement This:

- **Set standards for the women you date.** What qualities do you expect?
- **Never tolerate flakiness, drama, or disrespect.**
- **Don't be afraid to reject women who don't align with your values.**

Becoming the High-Value Man Women Chase

When you live with a **high-value mindset**, women will **instantly sense it.**

And here's the thing—**you don't have to tell women you're high-value.**

They'll just **feel it** in the way you:

✓ Carry yourself with confidence

✓ Prioritize your mission

✓ Refuse to chase or beg for attention

✓ Hold high standards for yourself and others

Women want a man who **knows his worth and owns his power.**

And when you **become that man**, you'll never have to convince a woman to like you.

Because she'll already know **you're the kind of man she doesn't want to lose.**

Chapter 5

Overcoming Fear of Rejection and Setbacks

Why Rejection is Inevitable (and Why That's a Good Thing)

Let's get real—**if you're putting yourself out there, you will face rejection.**

No matter how confident, attractive, or high-value you become, **not every woman will be interested in you.**

And that's **perfectly fine**—because rejection isn't about failure. **It's about filtering.**

Think about it this way:

- You wouldn't expect to walk into a store and have every single item be something you want to buy.
- You wouldn't expect to click on every show on Netflix and love all of them.

So why do men expect to be universally attractive to every woman they meet?

Rejection isn't a personal attack—it's just a sign that **she's not the right fit.**

And when you start seeing it that way, **it stops feeling like a big deal.**

The Real Reason Most Men Fear Rejection

Most guys aren't actually afraid of rejection itself—they're afraid of **what rejection means to them.**

For a low-confidence guy, rejection feels like:

"I'm not good enough."

"She's rejecting me because I lack something."

"This proves I'm not attractive to women."

For a high-value man, rejection feels like:

"We weren't a match, and that's okay."

"She didn't see my value—that's her loss."

"This has nothing to do with me personally."

The difference? **Perspective.**

Rejection doesn't define you—how you handle it does.

How to Overcome Rejection Like a High-Value Man

1. Stop Personalizing It

Rejection **isn't about you**—it's about **her preferences, circumstances, and emotions.**

Women reject men for countless reasons that have nothing to do with their worth:

- She just got out of a relationship.

- She's not in the mood to meet someone.
- She's dealing with personal issues.
- She's simply not attracted to you.

And that last one? **That's fine, too.**

Just like you're not attracted to every woman you meet, **she has her own taste.**

It's not a rejection of you as a person—**it's just a mismatch.**

Mindset Shift: When a woman rejects you, say to yourself, **"Cool, she's not my match. Moving on."**

2. Reframe Rejection as Proof You're Taking Action

Most men avoid rejection by **not approaching at all.**

But here's the reality—**if you're not getting rejected, you're not taking enough chances.**

Every rejection is **evidence that you're putting yourself out there.**

And every time you take a risk, you're **building confidence and experience.**

Action Step: Set a "Rejection Goal." Instead of fearing rejection, **aim to get rejected 10 times a week.**

- You'll quickly see that rejection isn't a big deal.
- You'll become more desensitized to it.
- And ironically—you'll start getting rejected **less** because you'll become more confident.

3. Detach Emotionally from the Outcome

Most men fear rejection because they **invest too much into one interaction.**

They walk up to a woman thinking:

- "I really hope this works."
- "I need her to like me."
- "This has to go well."

And because they **care too much about the result**, they put pressure on themselves—**and that pressure makes them nervous and awkward.**

A high-value man? **He doesn't care about the outcome.**

He knows:

- **There are plenty of women out there.**
- **If she's not interested, that's fine.**
- **Her reaction doesn't define his worth.**

Mindset Shift: Approach every woman with a "let's see if we vibe" mindset instead of a "please like me" mindset.

4. Turn Rejection into Growth

Rejection is only **painful if you don't learn from it.**

Instead of sulking, ask yourself:

- **"Did I approach with confidence?"**
- **"Did I maintain good eye contact and body language?"**

- **"Did I seem too nervous or unsure?"**
- **"Did I let her do most of the talking, or did I dominate the conversation?"**

Rejection is the best teacher. The more you analyze it, **the better you get.**

Action Step: After every rejection, write down one thing you can improve next time.

How to Handle a Harsh or Rude Rejection

Most rejections are **polite**—but every now and then, you'll meet a woman who's unnecessarily rude about it.

Here's how a low-value man reacts:

- **Gets defensive.** ("Wow, you don't have to be a bitch about it.")
- **Gets insecure.** ("Why do women always reject me?")
- **Gets discouraged.** ("I'm never approaching again.")

Here's how a high-value man reacts:

- **Laughs it off.** (Because he doesn't take it personally.)
- **Walks away with confidence.** ("Alright, have a good night.")
- **Moves on instantly.** (Because he knows one woman's bad attitude means nothing.)

Mindset Shift: Don't reward negativity with your energy. Walk away and keep your head high.

Your New Rejection-Proof Mindset

From now on, whenever you face rejection, remember these truths:

Rejection isn't personal—it's just a mismatch. The more you get rejected, the more confident you become.

You don't need every woman to like you—you only need the right one.

A man who doesn't fear rejection becomes unstoppable.

The moment you stop caring about rejection... is the moment you start winning.

Chapter 6

First Impressions – Making a Lasting Impact

Why First Impressions Matter More Than You Think

Let's be clear—**first impressions can make or break attraction.**

When you meet a woman for the first time, she **immediately** picks up on:

✓ Your confidence (or lack of it)

✓ Your energy and presence

✓ Your body language and tone of voice

And here's the kicker—**this all happens in the first few seconds.**

In fact, studies show that people form an impression of you **within the first 7 seconds of meeting you.**

If you don't make an impact right away, **you might not get a second chance.**

The good news? **You can control how people perceive you.**

If you master **how to make an unforgettable first impression**, women will feel naturally drawn to you—**before you even say a word.**

The 4 Pillars of an Irresistible First Impression

To make a powerful first impression, focus on these **four key areas:**

1. Strong, Confident Body Language

Before you speak, your body already communicates **who you are.**

Women instantly notice:

- **How you stand** (upright vs. slouched)
- **How you move** (relaxed vs. fidgety)
- **Your facial expressions** (calm vs. nervous)

How to Instantly Improve Your Presence:

✓ **Stand tall** with shoulders back—this signals confidence.

✓ **Walk with purpose**—don't shuffle or hesitate.

✓ **Slow down your movements**—rushed body language signals nervousness.

✓ **Hold eye contact**—but don't overdo it (relaxed, not creepy).

Pro Tip: The way you enter a room matters. **Walk in like you belong there.** Even if you don't feel 100% confident yet, **your body will train your mind to follow.**

2. A Powerful, Engaging Voice

Your voice **is just as important as your words.**

A high-value man speaks:

✓ **Slowly and deliberately**—he doesn't rush his words.
✓ **With a relaxed tone**—not too soft, not too aggressive.
✓ **With energy and warmth**—not flat or monotone.

How to Improve Your Voice Instantly:

✓ **Record yourself speaking** and analyze your tone.
✓ **Lower your pitch slightly**—higher voices can sound nervous.
✓ **Pause between sentences**—this makes you sound more in control.

Pro Tip: Speak as if you expect to be heard. The moment you **stop seeking approval in your voice**, people will automatically pay more attention to what you say.

3. A Magnetic Energy That Draws People In

Women are drawn to **energy.**

This doesn't mean you have to be the loudest guy in the room—**it means you have to bring a vibe that makes people want to be around you.**

- **Positive energy is contagious.** If you're excited, others will feel it.
- **Relaxed energy is magnetic.** If you're at ease, women will feel safe around you.

How to Cultivate an Attractive Energy:

✓ **Smile slightly when you enter a room**—not a forced grin, just a confident smirk.

✓ **Talk like you're enjoying yourself**—people mirror emotions.

✓ **Make people feel like you're happy to be there.**

Pro Tip: The easiest way to be charismatic? **Make others feel good in your presence.** If you make people feel comfortable, they'll naturally want to be around you.

4. Dressing Like a High-Value Man

Your style is a **silent introduction.**

Before a woman even speaks to you, she notices:

✓ The way your clothes fit

✓ Whether you take care of your appearance

✓ If you look put together or sloppy

How to Instantly Improve Your Style:

✓ **Wear clothes that fit well**—not too tight, not too baggy.

✓ **Stick to classic, well-fitted styles**—avoid flashy trends that don't suit you.

✓ **Groom yourself**—clean haircut, fresh breath, and a well-kept beard if you have one.

Pro Tip: You don't need expensive clothes to look sharp—**you just need clothes that fit well and make you feel confident.**

The "First 30 Seconds" Rule

If you want to leave a powerful impression, **the first 30 seconds of an interaction matter most.**

Here's what to do:

✓ **Approach with relaxed confidence**—no hesitation.

✓ **Make eye contact** and smile slightly.

✓ **Speak with warmth and certainty.**

✓ **Don't rush to impress**—let the conversation flow naturally.

Pro Tip: The best way to come across as high-status? **Act as if you're already comfortable with her presence.** This signals that you're confident and used to talking to attractive women.

How to Handle Nervousness When Meeting Women

Even if you **know all the right things to do**, you might still feel nervous. That's normal.

Here's how to manage it:

3 Quick Fixes for Nervousness:

✓ **Breathe deeply.** Nervousness comes from shallow breathing. Slow it down.

✓ **Pause before you speak.** Rushing makes you seem anxious.

✓ **Remind yourself that attraction is about energy—not perfection.**

Pro Tip: If you feel nervous, **shift your focus away from yourself and onto her.** Ask her a question and engage in what she's saying. This takes the pressure off you.

The Takeaway

Your first impression **sets the tone for attraction.**

If you master:

Confident body language

A strong, engaging voice

A positive, magnetic energy

A sharp, high-value style

…then you'll **stand out instantly.**

Women won't just notice you—they'll **feel drawn to you before you even say a word.**

And once you have that? **Everything else becomes easier.**

Chapter 7

The Art of Conversation – Building Instant Chemistry

Why Conversation is the Key to Attraction

You can look sharp, have strong body language, and radiate confidence—but if your conversation skills are weak, attraction **won't go anywhere.**

Think about it—what happens after a woman notices you?

She talks to you.

And in that moment, she's asking herself:

- "Does he excite me?"
- "Does he make me feel something?"
- "Is this conversation fun, engaging, or just boring?"

If your conversations **lack energy, depth, or intrigue,** she'll **lose interest fast.**

But if you can spark **chemistry**, make her **laugh**, and create an emotional connection, she'll **feel drawn to you**—and want more.

The good news? **Flawless conversation isn't something you're born with—it's a skill you can master.**

The 3 Levels of Conversation

Great conversations **flow naturally**, but behind the scenes, they follow a simple structure:

✓**Surface-Level Conversation** (Breaking the Ice)

✓**Emotional Connection** (Creating Chemistry)

✓**Flirtation & Attraction** (Building Tension)

Let's break each one down.

---

1. Surface-Level Conversation – Breaking the Ice

The first few minutes of a conversation **set the tone.**

Most guys overthink this part, trying to come up with the **perfect opening line.** But the truth is—**the words don't matter as much as your energy.**

How to Nail the First 30 Seconds:

✓ **Smile and make eye contact**—this instantly makes you more engaging.

✓ **Start with a casual opener.** The simpler, the better.
✓ **Match her energy.** If she's playful, be playful. If she's calm, ease into the vibe.

Great Openers That Feel Natural:

Situational Openers (Comment on something in the environment)

- "This place has the worst music, or is it just me?"
- "I swear I've seen you somewhere before. Wait, do you work for the FBI?"

Observational Openers (Make a playful guess about her)

- "You have the 'I pretend to be responsible but secretly cause trouble' look."
- "Let me guess—you're the kind of person who never texts back."

Simple, Direct Openers (Confident and no games)

- "You seem like fun. I'm [your name]."
- "I had to come say hi—you have a great energy."

Pro Tip: It's not about what you say—it's about how you say it. Say anything with **confidence and a smirk**, and it'll work.

---

2. Emotional Connection – Creating Chemistry

Once the conversation is flowing, your next job is to **make her feel something.**

Women don't remember **what you say**—they remember **how you make them feel.**

How to Create Instant Chemistry:

Tell engaging stories. Women love a man who can **paint a picture and bring emotion into a conversation.**
✓ **Ask deeper questions.** Avoid boring interview-style questions like "What do you do for work?"
✓ **Be playful and tease her.** Chemistry is built through **fun, flirtatious energy.**

Examples of Chemistry-Building Questions:

Fun & Playful:

- "On a scale from 1-10, how much of a troublemaker are you?"
- "What's something random you're ridiculously good at?"

Deep & Emotional:

- "What's one thing you've always wanted to do but haven't yet?"
- "What's the best spontaneous decision you've ever made?"

Pro Tip: The best way to keep her engaged? **Don't just ask—share your own fun answers, too.**

---

3. Flirtation & Attraction – Building Tension

Attraction **thrives on tension**—the push and pull between interest and mystery.

If you only have **nice, friendly conversations**, she may like you as a person but won't feel a spark.

Flirtation is what **separates friends from lovers.**

How to Flirt Like a Pro:

✓ **Tease her playfully**—lighthearted teasing creates tension and keeps things fun.

✓ **Use strong eye contact**—holding eye contact for an extra second creates excitement.

✓ **Drop subtle compliments**—but **not** the boring kind every guy gives.

Flirty Teasing Examples:

If she says she's good at something:

- "I don't know, I feel like you're hyping yourself up too much. I need proof."

If she does something clumsy:

- "Wow, smooth move. You're totally the most coordinated person here."

If she playfully challenges you:

- "Oh, so you think you're in charge here? That's cute."

Pro Tip: The secret to great flirting? **Stay relaxed, don't force it, and enjoy the moment.**

The #1 Mistake That Kills Attraction: Interview Mode

Most guys **ruin their conversations** because they ask questions like this:

"So, what do you do for work?"

"Where are you from?"

"Do you come here often?"

These questions aren't bad on their own, but they feel like an **interview**—not a fun, engaging experience.

Fix it with this simple trick:

Instead of just asking questions, **make statements and assumptions.**

"What do you do for work?"

"You have a lawyer vibe. Or are you secretly a criminal mastermind?"

"Where are you from?"

"Wait, don't tell me—you're totally from New York. I can tell by your attitude."

Pro Tip: Women love when a conversation feels **spontaneous and unpredictable.**

How to Never Run Out of Things to Say

One of the biggest fears men have is **awkward silences.**

Here's how to **keep the conversation flowing effortlessly:**

Use the "Story-Question-Statement" Formula:

Whenever she says something, respond in three steps:

Tell a short story related to it.

Ask her an open-ended question.

Make a fun statement to keep the energy up.

Example:

Her: "I just got back from a trip to Italy."

You:

"Italy is amazing! I went there last year, and I almost got lost in Venice." *(Short story)*

"What was your favorite part of the trip?" *(Open-ended question)*

"Wait, don't tell me—you were totally that tourist taking pictures of your food." *(Fun statement)*

Pro Tip: When you follow this structure, conversations flow naturally without ever feeling forced.

The Takeaway

Mastering conversation **isn't about saying the "right" thing—it's about creating a fun, engaging experience.**

✓ **Break the ice with confidence.**

✓ **Create chemistry through stories, humor, and deeper topics.**

✓ **Flirt playfully to build attraction and tension.**

✓ **Avoid "interview mode" and keep the conversation dynamic.**

When you get this right, women won't just enjoy talking to you—**they'll feel excited to see you again.**

Chapter 8

Understanding Female Psychology and Attraction Triggers

Why You Need to Understand Female Psychology

Most men struggle with women **because they don't understand how women think.**

They assume:
Women want the "nice guy" who treats them perfectly.
Attraction is purely logical.
If a woman likes you today, she'll like you forever.

But here's the truth: **Women are not attracted the same way men are.**

Men are **visually driven**—they see a beautiful woman and instantly feel attraction.
Women are **emotionally driven**—they are attracted to **how a man makes them feel.**

If you understand **how female attraction actually works**, you'll never be confused by:
✔ Why women like some guys and ignore others
✔ Why attraction can build over time (or vanish overnight)
✔ How to naturally make women feel drawn to you

Let's break it all down.

The 5 Attraction Triggers That Make Women Want You

1. Confidence (The Foundation of Attraction)

Confidence is the #1 thing that attracts women—period.

A man can be **average-looking**, but if he carries himself like he's valuable, women will **feel it**.

Women don't just see confidence—they **sense it** through:
✔ **Your body language** (Are you standing tall or shrinking?)
✔ **Your voice** (Do you speak with certainty or hesitation?)
✔ **How you handle challenges** (Do you stay calm under pressure?)

How to Instantly Signal Confidence:
✔ Hold eye contact **without looking away first.**
✔ Speak **slowly and deliberately**—rushed speech signals nervousness.
✔ Take up space—**don't shrink yourself in a room.**

Pro Tip: Women will "test" your confidence by teasing or challenging you. **Pass the test by staying relaxed, playful, and unfazed.**

---

2. Mystery & Unpredictability (The Spark of Excitement)

Women **love mystery.** If a woman can predict everything about you, attraction **fizzles out.**

Think about movies or TV shows—people stay engaged because **they don't know what's coming next.**

How to Add Mystery & Keep Her Hooked:
✓ **Don't reveal everything at once.** Let her be curious.
✓ **Avoid being overly available.** A busy man is attractive.
✓ **Be unpredictable in conversations.** Mix teasing with deeper topics.

Pro Tip: Never try to "convince" a woman to like you. Instead, **give her the fun of figuring you out.**

---

3. Status & Social Proof (Why Women Want Men Other Women Want)

Women are wired to be **attracted to high-status men.**

This doesn't mean you have to be rich or famous—it means:
✓ Other people respect you
✓ You carry yourself like you're valuable
✓ You have a life that excites you

How to Naturally Show Status:

✓ **Have a strong social circle.** Women notice when others enjoy your presence.

✓ **Don't be desperate.** The less you chase, the more valuable you seem.

✓ **Own your space.** High-status men **walk, talk, and move with certainty.**

Pro Tip: If you act like a man who already has options, women will assume you do.

---

4. Emotional Stimulation (Making Her Feel Something)

Women **don't fall for "nice guys"**—they fall for men who make them **feel something.**

The key to attraction? **Shifting her emotions.**

How to Keep Her Emotionally Engaged:

✓ **Use playful teasing.** Women love a guy who can challenge them in a fun way.

✓ **Tell stories with passion.** Emotionally engaging men are unforgettable.

✓ **Fluctuate between being serious and playful.** This keeps her hooked.

Pro Tip: The more emotions you make her feel, the **stronger the attraction becomes.**

5. Masculine Leadership (Taking Control of the Moment)

Women are naturally drawn to men who **lead.**

This doesn't mean being bossy—it means being **decisive, assertive, and in control.**

How to Show Leadership in Subtle Ways:

✓ **Make plans instead of asking what she wants.** ("We're going to check out this cool spot tonight.")

✓ **Take the lead in physical escalation.** Don't wait for her to make the first move.

✓ **Handle challenges calmly.** Women love a man who keeps his cool.

Pro Tip: When a woman feels like she can **trust your leadership**, attraction skyrockets.

What Women Say vs. What They Actually Respond To

Here's where most men get confused—**women don't always say what they actually respond to.**

Example 1:

What women say: "I just want a nice guy who treats me well."

What women respond to: A confident man with a backbone who doesn't put her on a pedestal.

Example 2:

What women say: "I like guys who are always honest about their feelings."

What women respond to: Men who **show their interest through action**, not needy words.

Example 3:

What women say: "I like a guy who's always available for me."

What women respond to: Men who have **their own lives and aren't always waiting around.**

The key takeaway? Women **aren't lying**—they just aren't always aware of what actually creates attraction. **Pay attention to what they respond to, not just what they say.**

How to Tell If She's Actually Attracted to You

Women won't always say, "I like you." Instead, they'll **drop subtle signals.**

Here's what to look for:

Signs She's Into You:
✓ **She mirrors your movements.** (Subconscious attraction cue.)
✓ **She makes playful physical contact.** (Touch is a strong signal.)
✓ **She finds excuses to keep talking.** (The longer she stays, the more she's into it.)

The Seduction Blueprint

✓ **She teases or challenges you.** (Testing your confidence.)

Signs She's NOT Interested:
She gives short, one-word answers.
She avoids eye contact or leans away.
She keeps checking her phone.
She doesn't ask any questions back.

Pro Tip: If a woman isn't showing signs of interest, **don't chase—just move on.** Confidence is knowing when to walk away.

The Takeaway

Understanding **female psychology** gives you a **huge advantage** in attraction.

If you master:
Confidence (Owning your value)
Mystery (Keeping her intrigued)
Social Proof (Being a man of value)
Emotional Stimulation (Making her feel something)
Masculine Leadership (Taking the lead with certainty)

…then **you'll never have to guess what women want again.**

Attraction isn't about memorizing lines or tricks—it's about **becoming a man women naturally gravitate toward.**

And once you get this? **Everything changes.**

Chapter 9

Where to Meet Women – High-Yield Environments for Connection

Why "Where" Matters Just as Much as "How"

You can have great conversation skills, confidence, and presence—but if you're always in the **wrong environments**, meeting women will feel like a struggle.

Think about it: If you're looking for quality women who share your interests, but you're only meeting people in loud, chaotic nightclubs… **you're setting yourself up for failure.**

That's why the key to success with women isn't just about **how you approach—it's about where you go.**

The right environments will:

✓ Make interactions feel **natural and effortless**
✓ Give you **shared interests** to bond over
✓ Help you meet **women who actually fit your lifestyle**

Let's break down **the best places to meet high-quality women**—and how to make the most of every opportunity.

The 3 Best Categories of Places to Meet Women

To maximize your success, you want to focus on places that:

✓ Have **a high volume of women**
✓ Encourage **natural interaction**
✓ Allow you to **stand out in a positive way**

Here are the best categories:

1. Social Events & Activity-Based Gatherings

Why It Works: Women are more open to meeting new people in fun, social environments where conversations flow naturally.

Best Places to Meet Women Socially:

✓ **Networking Events & Conferences** – Great for ambitious, high-value women.

✓ **Weddings & Private Parties** – Women are relaxed and open to meeting new people.

✓ **Dance Classes (Salsa, Bachata, Swing, etc.)** – Built-in physical connection & conversation.

✓ **Trivia Nights & Game Nights** – Easy way to connect in a playful, competitive setting.

✓ **Cooking or Wine Tasting Classes** – Women love these, and they're fun conversation starters.

Pro Tip: In social settings, the best way to meet women is to **own your space and have fun.** Don't focus on chasing—focus on being the guy who's already having a great time.

---

2. Daytime "Organic" Meeting Spots

Why It Works: Women are often more **open to genuine conversations** in non-bar settings where they don't feel like they're being hit on all the time.

Best Daytime Spots to Meet Women:
✓ **Cafés & Coffee Shops** – Easy to start casual, relaxed conversations.

✓ **Bookstores** – If you see a woman browsing a book, you instantly have a conversation starter.

✓ **Farmers Markets** – Social, friendly environment with built-in small talk opportunities.

✓ **Dog Parks** – If you have a dog, this is one of the easiest ways to meet women.

✓ **Gyms & Yoga Studios** (If done right) – Build familiarity first; don't be a creep.

Pro Tip: In daytime environments, your approach should be **casual and situational**—not overly direct. "Hey, I noticed you looking at that book. Have you read anything else by that author?" **feels natural, not forced.**

3. Nightlife & Social Venues (Without the Club Chaos)

Why It Works: Women go out to have fun, and **if you know how to navigate nightlife the right way, you can meet incredible women.**

Best Nightlife Spots That Aren't Just Loud Clubs:

✓ **Upscale Cocktail Bars** – Women dress up and expect to meet high-quality men.

✓ **Live Music Venues & Jazz Bars** – Laid-back, fun environment without the chaos.

✓ **Comedy Shows** – Laughter creates instant attraction and an easy conversation starter.

✓ **Hotel Lounges** – Classy, professional women often frequent these.

✓ **Wine Bars & Speakeasies** – Women love unique, intimate atmospheres.

Pro Tip: If you're going out at night, **skip the noisy clubs** and choose venues where conversation is actually possible.

How to Approach Women in Each Environment

Knowing **where to go** is half the battle—**but you also need to know how to approach in each setting.**

Social Gatherings & Events: Be the Social Connector

✓ Walk in **with positive energy**—people mirror emotions.
✓ Start by talking to **everyone**, not just attractive women.
✓ Use **group conversation skills**—engage the whole group first.

Best Approach Example:

- "Hey, I don't know many people here—what's the best way to survive this party?" (Playful, non-threatening, and invites a fun response.)

Daytime Settings: Keep It Casual & Light

✓ Approach with **a relaxed, non-needy vibe.**
✓ Use **situational openers** based on the environment.
✓ If she's busy, **keep it short and direct.**

Best Approach Example (Coffee Shop):

- "You look like you've got great taste in coffee. What's your go-to order?" (Fun, easy way to start a conversation.)

Nightlife Settings: Bring the Right Energy

✓ Avoid being the guy who **just scans for women**—actually enjoy yourself.
✓ Position yourself **near the bar or high-traffic areas.**

✓ If a woman is in a group, **talk to her friends first before focusing on her.**

Best Approach Example (Cocktail Bar):
- "Alright, serious question—on a scale of 1 to 10, how strong is this bartender's drink game?" (Playful, fun, and keeps the conversation moving.)

The #1 Mistake Most Guys Make When Trying to Meet Women

Most men **only meet women in bars and nightclubs**—and then wonder why they struggle to make real connections.

If you only meet women in chaotic, drunk environments, you'll only attract women who fit that setting.

High-value men meet women **in places that align with their lifestyle.**

Pro Tip: Think about the **type of woman you want to attract**, then **go to places where those kinds of women naturally are.**

How to Expand Your Social Circle & Meet More Women Effortlessly

One of the easiest ways to **attract more women without chasing** is to **build a strong social circle.**

The Seduction Blueprint

Here's how:

1. Get into high-value social circles.

✓ Join exclusive social groups, masterminds, or networking events.

✓ Say yes to invites and introduce yourself to new people.

2. Become the guy who hosts events.

✓ Throw small house parties, game nights, or dinner gatherings.

✓ Women love being invited to fun, well-organized events.

3. Surround yourself with women (even as friends).

✓ When women see you with **other women**, they naturally assume you're valuable.

✓ Women introduce you to **other women**—social proof is powerful.

Pro Tip: When you **focus on building a great social life**, meeting women becomes **effortless**.

The Takeaway

Attraction isn't just about what you say—it's about **where you position yourself.**

If you focus on:

Social Events & Activities (Fun, natural settings)

Daytime Organic Meetups (Easy, casual interactions)

High-Quality Nightlife Spots (Where real conversations can happen)

…then **you'll meet amazing women effortlessly.**

Stop wasting time in places that don't align with you. **Put yourself in the right environments, and the right women will follow.**

Chapter 10

How to Flirt and Create Romantic Tension

Why Flirting is the Key to Attraction

Flirting **separates friends from lovers.**

You can be confident, well-dressed, and a great conversationalist, but if you don't know how to **create tension and playful attraction,** you'll end up as…

☠ The "nice guy" she likes but isn't attracted to.

Women **need excitement, mystery, and playful push-pull dynamics** to feel drawn toward a man.

Flirting is what makes her heart race. It's what makes her think about you **long after the conversation ends.**

The best part? **Flirting is a skill that anyone can learn.**

Let's break down how to do it right.

The 4 Pillars of Great Flirting

1. **Playful Teasing** (Challenge her in a fun way)
2. **Strong Eye Contact** (Create tension without words)
3. **Physical Escalation** (Build excitement through touch)
4. **Push-Pull Dynamics** (The dance of attraction)

Let's go through each one.

---

1. Playful Teasing – Make Her Laugh & Chase You

Flirting is **playful, not serious.** It's about having fun, not proving yourself.

How to Tease Women the Right Way:

✓ Make **light, playful jokes about her** (never be mean or insulting).

✓ Challenge her in a way that **sparks excitement**.

✓ Flip the script—**make her qualify herself to you.**

Examples of Playful Teasing:

If she says she's good at something:

- "Mmm, I don't know, I feel like you're hyping yourself up too much. I need proof."

If she's wearing glasses:

- "You're trying to look all sophisticated, but I can tell you're secretly trouble."

If she's playfully challenging you:

- "Oh, you think you're in charge here? That's cute."

Pro Tip: Women **love** a man who makes them laugh and **keeps them on their toes.**

---

2. Strong Eye Contact – Creating Tension Without Words

Want to instantly create attraction? Hold eye contact.

Most men break eye contact too soon because they feel uncomfortable.

But when you hold eye contact confidently, it builds tension.

How to Use Eye Contact to Flirt:

✓ When talking to her, **hold her gaze slightly longer than normal.**

✓ If she looks away, **keep holding it until she looks back.**

✓ Add a slight smirk—it makes the moment **playful and exciting.**

Pro Tip: If she holds eye contact and smiles, **she's into you.**

---

3. Physical Escalation – Flirting Through Touch

Touch is one of the strongest ways to build attraction.

But most men make one of two mistakes:
They don't touch at all (afraid of being "creepy").
They go too far too fast (making her uncomfortable).

The key? **Start small and build up.**

How to Flirt with Touch (The Right Way):

✔ **Light touches early on** – A playful tap on the arm when laughing.

✔ **Gradual escalation** – Hand on her lower back when leading her somewhere.

✔ **Match her response** – If she touches you back, she's comfortable.

Golden Rule: Touch should feel natural, not forced. If she leans into it, keep going. If she pulls away, slow down.

---

4. Push-Pull Dynamics – The Dance of Attraction

Flirting is a game of tension. If you give a woman too much attention **too soon**, she loses interest.

The secret? **Push-Pull.**

**Push = Playfully challenge her, tease her, or pull away.
Pull = Give her attention, compliment her, or engage warmly.**

Examples of Push-Pull Flirting:

Push:

- "You're kind of trouble—I don't know if I should be talking to you."

Pull:

- "But you do have a cute smile… so maybe I'll take the risk."

Push:

- "I don't think we can be friends—you're way too competitive."

Pull:

- "But I do like your energy. You'd be fun to have around."

Pro Tip: The goal of push-pull is to keep her **emotionally engaged.** If you're too predictable, attraction dies.

The #1 Flirting Mistake That Kills Attraction

Being too available.

Most men **give too much, too soon**—compliments, attention, validation.

Women don't want a guy who chases—they want a guy they have to earn.

Fix this by:

✓ Giving **playful push-pull interactions** instead of constant compliments.

✓ Letting **her invest in the conversation**—don't do all the work.

✓ Keeping a little **mystery**—don't reveal everything at once.

Pro Tip: Attraction isn't about proving yourself—it's about **making her want to prove herself to you.**

How to Tell If She's Flirting Back

Women **flirt in subtle ways.** If you know the signs, you'll never second-guess her interest.

Signs She's Flirting Back:

✓ She **laughs at your jokes** (even the bad ones).

✓ She **touches you back** or gets physically close.

✓ She **teases you playfully** (flipping your jokes back at you).

✓ She **holds eye contact and smirks**.

✓ She **finds ways to keep the conversation going.**

If she's doing these things? She's into you.

Pro Tip: If she's not flirting back, **don't force it—just move on.** Confidence is knowing when to walk away.

The Takeaway

Flirting is **the spark that turns conversations into attraction.**

If you master:
Playful teasing (Keeping it fun and exciting)
Strong eye contact (Creating tension without words)
Physical escalation (Building chemistry naturally)
Push-pull dynamics (The dance of attraction)

…then **you'll create deep, effortless attraction—without ever chasing.**

Flirting is what makes a woman crave your attention.
Master it, and you'll stand out from 99% of men.

Chapter 11

How to Navigate Group Dynamics and Social Proof

Why Social Proof is One of the Most Powerful Attraction Triggers

Women **don't just notice you—they notice how others react to you.**

If you walk into a room and people **light up, laugh at your jokes, and respect your presence**, women will **instantly** assume you're valuable.

This is called **social proof**—and it's one of the most powerful attraction triggers.

Women are biologically wired to be attracted to men who are liked and respected by others.

It's not just about **what you say**—it's about how you're **perceived in a social setting.**

If you can navigate **group dynamics effectively**, you'll:

✓ Stand out naturally, without trying too hard.

✓ Get **women approaching you**, instead of chasing them.

✓ Become **magnetic** in any social environment.

Let's break it all down.

The 3 Laws of Social Proof & Group Attraction

1. **Women are drawn to men who are liked by others.**
2. **Being good with groups makes you stand out effortlessly.**
3. **The way you interact with others changes how women perceive you.**

Now, let's break down **how to dominate group settings like a high-status man.**

1. How to Become Instantly High-Status in a Group

When you enter a room, **people subconsciously decide your value based on three things:**

✓ **Your energy** – Are you relaxed, confident, and engaging?

✓ **How others react to you** – Do people respect and enjoy your presence?

✓ **Your body language** – Do you take up space and own the moment?

How to Command Respect in Any Group Setting:

✓ **Smile and be the source of good energy.** People mirror emotions.

✓ **Don't rush to impress—let the conversation flow to you.**

✓ **Engage with everyone, not just attractive women.**

Golden Rule: Women notice the man who **controls the room without needing to be loud.**

---

2. How to Approach a Group the Right Way

Most guys mess up when they approach a group because they:
Ignore the friends and go straight for the woman they're interested in.

Act nervous and wait for permission to speak. Interrupt the flow instead of smoothly joining in.

How to Enter a Group & Get Accepted Instantly:

✓ **Start by engaging the whole group—not just the woman you like.**

✓ **Make a positive observation about the group dynamic.**

✓ **Ease into the conversation instead of forcing your way in.**

Example Group Entry Approaches:

At a bar or social event:

- "Alright, I have to ask—who's the troublemaker of the group?" (Playful, includes everyone.)

If they're laughing at something:

- "I don't know what's happening, but it looks way too fun to not be involved."

If you already know someone in the group:

- "Hey [friend's name], are you corrupting these fine people or are they corrupting you?"

Golden Rule: If you make **the group like you first**, the woman you're interested in will naturally become curious about you.

---

3. How to Win Over the "Gatekeeper" Friend

In every group, there's usually a **dominant personality**—the person who sets the tone for the group.

If you win over the leader, the rest of the group (including the women) will accept you easily.

This could be:

✓ The most outgoing friend.
✓ The overprotective best friend.
✓ The social organizer who planned the event.

How to Win Over the Group Leader:

✓ **Respect their role** – Don't challenge them—make them your ally.

✓ **Include them in jokes & conversations.**

✓ **Compliment them subtly.** ("This crew is awesome—you must be the ringleader.")

Golden Rule: Women feel safer engaging with you if their friends approve of you.

---

4. How to Flirt in a Group Without Making It Awkward

The key to flirting in a group setting? **Subtlety.**

If you **zero in on a woman too soon**, it can feel forced or make her uncomfortable.

How to Flirt in a Group Smoothly:

✓ **Start by engaging the group**—let her see you're fun.

✓ **Give her playful attention in a way that doesn't exclude others.**

✓ **Use light physical touch in moments where it feels natural.**

Example:
If the group is discussing something funny, you can lightly touch her arm and say:

- "I feel like you're way too innocent for this conversation." (*Teasing, fun, and subtle.*)

Pro Tip: The best way to flirt in a group is to **create a fun atmosphere, then let her come to you.**

5. How to Use Social Proof to Make Women Chase You

The more people like and respect you, the more attractive you become.

Women **pay attention** to:
✓ How people react to you.
✓ How comfortable you are in social situations.
✓ Whether other women are interested in you.

How to Boost Your Social Proof Instantly:

✓ **Be surrounded by people.** If you walk into a bar alone and stand in the corner, women will assume you're low-status.

✓ **Have female friends.** Women love men who are socially comfortable around other women.

✓ **Make people laugh and have fun.** Women love men who bring good energy.

Pro Tip: Women are naturally attracted to men who **don't "need" their attention but already have social value.**

The #1 Mistake That Kills Your Social Proof

Being too focused on one woman too soon.

Most men make the mistake of:

Ignoring the group and only talking to the girl they like.

The Seduction Blueprint

Getting possessive and hovering over her.

Getting quiet and awkward when she talks to other people.

The key? Be socially valuable to everyone.

Fix it by:

✓ Talking to **everyone in the group first.**

✓ Making sure **you're adding energy to the whole vibe.**

✓ Letting **her feel like she's earning your attention.**

Pro Tip: The man who can hold the attention of an entire group is the man women will chase.

The Takeaway

If you master **group dynamics**, you become:

A man who naturally stands out in social settings. Someone women **want to be around** because they see others drawn to you.

A guy who **never has to chase**—because **attraction happens naturally.**

When you become the high-status man in the group, women will want to be part of your world.

Chapter 12

The Art of Getting Her Number and Following Up

Why Most Men Fail at Getting a Woman's Number

Getting a woman's number **shouldn't feel like a big deal**—but most men either:

Ask too soon, before any real connection is built.
Wait too long, causing the moment to fizzle out.
Make it awkward, turning what should be smooth into a high-pressure situation.

Here's the truth: **If the conversation is going well, getting her number should feel like the next natural step.**

Let's break down **exactly how to do it effortlessly—without awkwardness or fear of rejection.**

The 3 Golden Rules for Getting Her Number

1. Make the interaction fun first. (A number means nothing without chemistry.)

2. Lead confidently. (If you're unsure, she'll hesitate.)

3. Set up a reason for future contact. (Give her a reason to say yes.)

Now, let's go deeper.

---

1. When is the Right Time to Ask for Her Number?

You should ask **when there's a natural high point in the conversation**—not after a long pause or when things start to die down.

Best Moments to Ask:

✔ **After you've shared a fun moment together.** (Laughter is the best sign.)

✔ **When you've discovered a mutual interest.** (Shared hobbies, events, travel plans.)

✔ **Before leaving the interaction on a high note.** (Never wait until things get dull.)

Pro Tip: If you ask for her number **after a strong moment**, she's more likely to associate you with fun and say yes.

---

2. The Best Way to Ask for Her Number (Without Being Awkward)

The key? Make it feel effortless.

Weak & Uncertain: "Uh… so… can I have your number?" (Sounds needy.)

Overly Formal: "Would it be okay if I got your contact information?" (Too stiff.)

Confident & Smooth: "We should continue this conversation later—what's your number?"

Casual & Playful Approaches That Work:

✓ **The "Let's See If We Get Along" Approach:**
- "You seem fun. I'll have to test that theory—drop me your number."

✓ **The "Let's Continue This" Approach:**
- "We're definitely getting drinks sometime. What's your number?"

✓ **The "Challenge" Approach:**
- "I feel like you're an interesting mix of trouble and fun. I might need your number to confirm."

Pro Tip: Never phrase it as a question—state it as if it's the next logical step.

---

3. What to Do If She Hesitates

Sometimes, a woman will hesitate or say, "I don't usually give my number out."

Most guys **panic** and either:

Get defensive. ("Oh, okay, never mind...")

Start convincing her. ("But I'm a nice guy, I swear!")

The confident move? Stay cool and unfazed.

How to Handle Resistance Smoothly:

Her: "I don't usually give out my number."

You: "Ah, so you're saying I have to earn it? I like a challenge." (*Playful, keeps the energy high.*)

Her: "I don't know… I just met you."

You: "Exactly! That's why we should continue this later." (*Confident, frames it as a no-brainer.*)

Pro Tip: If she's unsure, don't push—just say, "No worries," and move on. Confidence is knowing when to walk away.

The Follow-Up: How to Text Her the Right Way

Getting her number is just the first step—how you text determines whether she actually responds.

Most men either:

Text too soon. ("Had fun talking to you!!") – Comes off eager.
Wait too long. (3+ days of silence.) – Feels like you forgot about her.
Send a boring first message. ("Hey, what's up?") – No excitement, no spark.

The Best Way to Text First:

1. Reference a fun moment from your conversation.

- "I still can't believe you've never seen [movie name]. We might need to fix that."

2. Keep it light and playful.
- "I feel like you're secretly competitive. I might have to challenge you to [activity]."

3. Be direct about plans.
- "Let's grab drinks this week. Are you more of a whiskey or wine person?"

Pro Tip: If she takes a while to reply, **don't double-text or act needy.** Confidence is knowing she'll respond when she's free.

What to Do If She Doesn't Respond

If she doesn't reply after 1-2 days:

✓ **Stay cool—don't panic or overthink.**

✓ **Send one light follow-up a couple of days later.** (Something playful, not needy.)

Good Follow-Up Example:
- "Alright, I'll take that silence as you planning a grand entrance for your reply." (*Playful, gives her a chance to re-engage.*)

What NOT to Do:
- "Hey? Did you get my last message?" (Too needy.)
- "Guess you're not interested…" (Passive-aggressive.)

Golden Rule: If she ignores your follow-up? **Move on. Confidence is knowing when to stop chasing.**

How to Set Up the First Date Over Text

Your goal is to move from texting to real life—quickly.

Most guys kill attraction by:

Texting back and forth for days without making plans.
Asking **her** to decide what to do. ("What do you want to do?")
Being too vague. ("Wanna hang out sometime?")

How to Set Up a Date Smoothly:

1. Pick a specific time & place.

- "Let's grab a drink this Thursday at [cool spot]. You in?"

2. Make it casual, not a big deal.

- "Let's get coffee and make fun of people who take coffee too seriously."

3. If she hesitates, stay playful.

- "Okay, I get it. You're playing hard to get. I respect the strategy."

Pro Tip: High-value men don't waste time on endless texting—they lead the interaction toward a real meet-up.

The #1 Mistake That Kills Your Chances After Getting Her Number

Being too available.

Women are drawn to men who have options and a life they're excited about.

How to Show You're High-Value Over Text:

✓ **Don't always reply instantly.** (Match her response time.)
✓ **Don't be the only one initiating.** (She should invest, too.)
✓ **If she cancels or flakes, don't chase—let her come back to you.**

Pro Tip: Women respect a man who **values his time**. If she's flaky, don't get upset—just move on.

The Takeaway

Getting her number is easy when you do it the right way.

If you master:

Asking at the right moment (During a high point in conversation)
Making it feel natural & confident (No hesitation, no pressure)
Following up with fun, engaging texts (No boring "Hey" messages)
Setting up the date quickly (Lead, don't text endlessly)

…then you'll **turn numbers into real connections effortlessly.**

Confidence isn't about getting every woman's number—it's about knowing you have the skill to attract the right ones.

Chapter 13

Planning and Leading Memorable Dates

Why Most Dates Fail (And How to Avoid It)

Most men **fail at dating not because women don't like them—but because their dates are boring, predictable, or lack excitement.**

The typical "dinner and a movie" date? **Forget it.**

Women don't want just another date—they want an experience that excites them.

A great date makes a woman feel:

✓ **Emotionally engaged** – Not just another "nice conversation."

✓ **A sense of adventure** – Something she hasn't done a hundred times before.

✓ **Attracted to you** – Not just "having fun" but feeling drawn to you.

Let's break down **how to plan dates that make women want more.**

The 3 Golden Rules of a Memorable Date

1. The man leads the date. (Confidence is attractive.)

2. The date should create emotional spikes. (Excitement, laughter, tension.)

3. The goal isn't just to spend time—it's to build attraction.

Now, let's break down exactly **how to do it right.**

Step 1: How to Choose the Perfect Date Spot

Best First Date Ideas That Work Every Time:

✓ **Cocktail Bars / Speakeasies** – Classy, relaxed, easy for conversation.

✓ **Rooftop Bars / Scenic Views** – Built-in atmosphere for romance.

✓ **Comedy Shows** – Laughter is one of the strongest attraction triggers.

✓ **Food Truck Parks / Outdoor Markets** – Casual, interactive, and easy-going.

✓ **Mini-Golf / Bowling / Arcade Bars** – Creates fun competition & playfulness.

Why These Work: They allow for **physical movement, interaction, and easy conversation.**

The Seduction Blueprint

Pro Tip: Avoid dinner as a first date—**it's too formal, too interview-like, and locks you in for too long.**

Step 2: How to Lead the Date Like a High-Value Man

Women are attracted to men who take charge.

How to Show Leadership on a Date:

✓ **Have a plan before she asks.** ("We're meeting at [cool spot] at 8.")
✓ **Guide her smoothly.** ("Follow me, I know a great spot.")
✓ **Handle logistics.** (Choose the place, get the drinks, lead the way.)

Pro Tip: Women feel attraction when a man **makes decisions effortlessly.**

Step 3: How to Build Chemistry and Emotional Connection

Women don't fall for facts—they fall for how you make them feel.

How to Build Chemistry on a Date:

✓ **Tease and playfully challenge her.** (Flirt, don't interview.)
✓ **Ask deeper questions.** ("What's the craziest thing you've ever done?")

✓ **Use storytelling.** (Talk about your passions & experiences with emotion.)

Avoid These Common Mistakes:

Talking about negative topics (Exes, work drama, politics). Over-sharing personal problems (She's not your therapist). Making the date too serious—keep it **fun, light, and flirty.**

Pro Tip: Your energy sets the tone—if you're having fun, she will too.

Step 4: The Art of Touch – Creating Physical Attraction

Touch is what separates "friend zone" from attraction.

How to Introduce Touch Naturally:

✓ **Light touches early on** – A playful tap on the arm when laughing.

✓ **Guiding her** – Placing a hand on her lower back when leading.

✓ **Escalating slowly** – If she's comfortable, move to more intimate touch (holding hands, brushing her hair back).

Pro Tip: If she touches you back, that's a **huge sign she's interested.**

Step 5: How to End the Date with Maximum Attraction

Most men fail at closing the date correctly.

How to End the Date the Right Way:

✓ **End on a high note.** (Don't drag the date out—leave her wanting more.)

✓ **If the vibe is right, go for the kiss.** (Watch for signs: eye contact, body language, closeness.)

✓ **Set up the next meeting instead of "let's hang out sometime."** ("Let's grab drinks Thursday—you free?")

Pro Tip: Confidence is everything. If you hesitate, she will too.

What to Do If She's Hesitant or Unsure

Sometimes a woman might:

Hesitate to make plans.

Be slow to respond to texts after the date.

Not show strong interest even if the date seemed good.

The key? Don't panic—just mirror her energy.

How to Handle Hesitation Smoothly:

✓ **If she's slow to respond, match her pace.** (Don't chase.)

✓ **If she seems unsure about another date, stay playful.** ("I see how it is… you're playing hard to get. I respect it.")

✓ **If she flakes, don't get upset—just move on.** ("No worries, let me know when you're free.")

Pro Tip: Women respect men who stay cool, confident, and unfazed.

The #1 Mistake That Kills Attraction on a Date

Being too agreeable.

Women don't want a guy who agrees with everything they say.

Fix it by:

✓ **Having opinions.** (It's okay to disagree—just do it playfully.)

✓ **Being willing to challenge her.** ("Wait, are you telling me you actually believe that?")

✓ **Not over-validating.** (Compliments are fine, but don't overdo it.)

Pro Tip: Attraction thrives on **a little playful tension.**

How to Make Sure She Wants a Second Date

Women don't want "just another date"—they want a feeling.

How to Make Her Excited for the Next Date:
✓ **End the first date with a fun "inside joke."**

(Something you two laughed about.)

✓ **Leave some mystery.** ("I'll tell you the rest of that crazy story next time.")

✓ **Text her something light and fun after the date.** ("I think you might be even cooler than I expected... but I need more evidence.")

Pro Tip: Women don't obsess over a man **because of what he says**—**they obsess because of how he made them feel.**

The Takeaway

A great date isn't just about "hanging out"—it's about creating attraction.

If you master:

Choosing the right date spots (Fun, interactive, and engaging)
Leading with confidence (Women want a man who takes charge)
Building emotional chemistry (Excitement, laughter, and intrigue)
Escalating physically the right way (From light touch to deep attraction)

...then **women will not only enjoy their time with you—they'll crave more.**

Dates aren't about impressing her—they're about making her feel something unforgettable.

Chapter 14

Building Emotional and Physical Connection

Why Emotional and Physical Connection Are the Keys to Deep Attraction

Most men focus only on **one side of attraction**—either trying to be emotionally connected (**"nice guys"**) or focusing purely on the physical (**"players"**).

The secret to deep attraction? Mastering both.

A woman needs to feel:

✓ **Emotionally connected** – She trusts you, enjoys talking to you, and feels safe.

✓ **Physically attracted** – She feels drawn to you, excited, and desires touch.

When you combine these two? **She won't be able to stop thinking about you.**

Let's break down exactly **how to create both emotional and physical attraction effortlessly.**

Step 1: Building Emotional Connection

Emotional connection makes her feel close to you—it's what makes attraction last.

But **most men do this wrong** by:

Acting like her therapist (boring, no attraction).

Being too logical (no emotional spark).

Oversharing personal struggles (too much, too soon).

How to Build Emotional Connection the Right Way:

1. Get Her to Open Up About Herself

- People feel closest to those they **share personal thoughts with.**
- Women connect deeply through **storytelling and shared emotions.**

Example Questions That Build Connection:

- "What's something you've always wanted to do but never have?"
- "What's the best spontaneous decision you've ever made?"
- "What's a moment in your life you'll never forget?"

2. Share Personal Stories That Show Your Depth

- Instead of just asking questions, **open up with your own stories.**

- Share **fun, emotional, or meaningful experiences**—things that shaped you.

Example:
Her: "I've always wanted to go skydiving but never have."
You: "I did it once! I was terrified at first, but the rush was unreal. You'd love it."

Pro Tip: Women don't fall for facts—they fall for emotions.

Step 2: Creating Physical Connection & Attraction

Physical touch is what separates a friend from a lover.

Most guys mess this up by:
Waiting too long (friend zone).
Going too fast (creepy).
Overthinking it (hesitation kills attraction).

How to Introduce Touch Naturally:

1. Start Small & Playful

✓ Lightly touch her arm when joking.

✓ Guide her by the lower back when leading her somewhere.

✓ Playfully push her away when teasing her.

2. Escalate Based on Her Response

- If she **leans in or touches you back** → She's comfortable—keep going.

- If she **pulls away or stiffens up** → Slow down, focus on emotional connection first.

How to Know She Wants More Touch:

✓ She **finds excuses to touch you.**

✓ She **mirrors your body language.**

✓ She **gets close to you without pulling away.**

Pro Tip: Women won't say, "Please touch me." They **signal it through body language**—pay attention!

Step 3: Building Sexual Tension (The Key to Intense Attraction)

Sexual tension is what makes her crave your touch.

Most guys ruin this by:
Rushing into touching too soon.
Being too hesitant or acting nervous.
Treating attraction like a logical process.

How to Create Sexual Tension the Right Way:

1. Hold Eye Contact & Pause Before Speaking

- A few seconds of **silence with deep eye contact** creates a powerful moment.
- If she smiles or blushes, **she's feeling it.**

2. Use Your Voice to Build Intrigue

- Slow down your speech—**a deep, controlled voice is attractive.**

- Drop your tone slightly when saying something intimate.

3. Tease Her Playfully About Attraction

Example:

- "I feel like you're pretending to be all innocent, but I don't believe it." (*Playful, flirty, and creates tension.*)

Pro Tip: The key to sexual tension is **leaving room for anticipation.**

Step 4: The Moment of the First Kiss

Most men mess this up by either:
Asking, "Can I kiss you?" (Kills the moment.)
Hesitating too long (She loses interest.)
Rushing it when the vibe isn't right.

How to Go for the Kiss Smoothly:

1. Read the Signs That She's Ready:
✓ She's holding strong eye contact and smiling.
✓ She's playing with her hair or biting her lip.
✓ She's moving closer to you, not pulling away.

2. Slow Down & Let the Tension Build

- Hold eye contact.
- Pause the conversation.
- Move slightly closer.

3. If She's Giving the Right Signals, Go for It

- Lean in **slowly and confidently**—not suddenly.
- If she leans in too, **it's on.**

Golden Rule: If you're unsure whether she's ready—**slow down, build more tension, and then go for it.**

The #1 Mistake That Kills Emotional & Physical Connection

Being Too Available & Predictable.

Women love men who keep a little mystery.

Fix this by:

✓ Not revealing everything about yourself too soon.

✓ Not being too eager—let her wonder about you.

✓ Keeping her on her toes with playful teasing.

Pro Tip: Tension is what keeps attraction alive—don't rush to "seal the deal" too soon.

The Takeaway

Women crave men who make them feel both emotionally & physically connected.

If you master:

Building emotional trust & chemistry (Sharing deep, fun, and engaging conversations)

Using natural touch & body language (Escalating attraction smoothly)

Creating sexual tension (Making her anticipate your next move)

Going for the kiss confidently (Reading her signals & leading the moment)

…then **you'll build a deep, unforgettable connection—one that keeps her coming back for more.**

The key isn't just attraction—it's making her feel something real.

Chapter 15

Handling Rejection and Keeping High Standards

Why Rejection is a Good Thing

Most men fear rejection. They see it as:

A sign they're not good enough.

A personal failure.

Something to be avoided at all costs.

But the truth? Rejection is one of the most powerful tools for growth and success with women.

Here's why:

✓ **Rejection filters out the wrong people.** Not every woman is the right fit for you.

✓ **Rejection means you're taking action.** The more you put yourself out there, the more success you'll have.

✓ **Handling rejection well makes you more attractive.** Women respect a man who isn't shaken by setbacks.

If you know how to **handle rejection the right way**, it stops being scary—and actually **boosts your confidence.**

The 3 Mindset Shifts That Make Rejection Meaningless

1. Rejection is NOT personal.

- Most of the time, rejection has **nothing to do with you.**
- She might be in a bad mood, in a relationship, or just not looking for anyone.
- **Her reaction does not define your value.**

Mindset Shift: Instead of thinking, "She rejected me," think: **"We weren't a match. Next."**

2. Every "No" Brings You Closer to a "Yes."

- Even the most attractive, confident men get rejected—it's part of the process.
- **The more you practice, the better you get.**
- If you get rejected 9 times but succeed once, **you're winning.**

Mindset Shift: Reframe rejection as progress. Every approach makes you stronger.

3. Women Test Men to See How They Handle Rejection.

- Sometimes, a woman will reject you **just to see how you react.**
- If you get upset or needy, you fail the test.

- If you stay calm, laugh it off, and move on—**you look like a high-status man.**

Mindset Shift: Confidence isn't never getting rejected—it's handling rejection without losing your power.

Pro Tip: Women are **attracted to men who don't let rejection shake them.**

How to Handle Rejection Like a High-Value Man

If she rejects you outright:

Her: "I'm not really interested."

You: "No worries! Have a great night." (*Confident, no emotional reaction.*)

If she hesitates but doesn't completely shut you down:
Her: "I don't usually give out my number."
You: "Ah, so you like to make guys work for it. I respect that." (*Playful, keeps the energy high.*)

Golden Rule: If she's firm in her rejection, **don't argue, beg, or convince her—just move on.**

Pro Tip: The man who can walk away **with confidence** instantly becomes more attractive.

The #1 Mistake That Makes Rejection Worse

Reacting emotionally.

Most guys:

Get upset and insult the woman. ("Whatever, you're not even that hot.")

Beg for another chance. ("Come on, just give me a shot!") Take it personally. ("I'll never be good with women.")

High-value men NEVER react emotionally to rejection.

How to Stand Out:

✔ **Stay cool and relaxed.** (Like it's no big deal.)
✔ **Keep smiling.** (Rejection doesn't affect your mood.)
✔ **Move on instantly.** (Plenty of other women out there.)

Pro Tip: The moment you stop fearing rejection, **your confidence skyrockets.**

How to Develop High Standards (And Make Women Work for You)

Most men accept any woman who shows interest.

- They **lower their standards** out of fear of being alone.
- They **chase women who treat them poorly.**
- They **put women on a pedestal instead of assessing if she's actually right for them.**

High-Value Men Think Differently:
✔ **They choose women who meet their standards.**
✔ **They walk away from disrespect or bad behavior.**
✔ **They don't chase—they attract.**

The 3 Signs of a High-Value Woman

1. She Brings More Than Just Looks

- A high-value woman **adds to your life**—mentally, emotionally, and socially.
- She has goals, passions, and a life outside of just "being attractive."
- If her only quality is "being hot," **you'll lose interest fast.**

2. She Respects Your Time and Effort

- A quality woman **doesn't play games** or flake last minute.
- She **values your time** and makes an effort to see you.
- If she's constantly flaking or being hot and cold? **Move on.**

3. She Supports and Challenges You

- The best relationships are with women who **push you to be better.**
- A great woman will challenge you **in a way that makes you stronger.**

Pro Tip: Attraction isn't just about finding a beautiful woman—it's about finding a **quality** woman.

How to Make Women Work for Your Attention

Women respect men they have to earn.

Most guys **do all the chasing**—which makes them look low-value.

How to Flip the Script:

✓ **Don't always be available.** Have a life you're passionate about.

✓ **Make her invest in the conversation.** Don't do all the work.

✓ **If she plays games, match her energy—or walk away.**

Examples of Making Her Work for It:

Her: *"Why don't you text me first?"*

You: "Because I like women who take initiative. You qualify." (*Playful, high-status response.*)

Her: *"Why should I go on a date with you?"*

You: "Good question. Let's see if you can keep up with me first." (*Challenge her to step up.*)

Pro Tip: The moment you stop acting like she's a prize—and start treating yourself like one—**everything changes.**

The Takeaway

Rejection isn't a problem—it's part of the process.

If you master:

Handling rejection with confidence (No emotional reactions, no fear)

Developing high standards (Choosing women who deserve you)

Making women work for you (Flipping the script, making her chase)

…then **you become the man that women respect, admire, and desire.**

Confidence isn't about avoiding rejection—it's about being unfazed by it.

Chapter 16

Turning a Date into a Meaningful Relationship (or Casual Encounter)

The Difference Between a Casual Fling and a Serious Relationship

The mistake most men make? They let women decide what the relationship will be.

High-value men **lead.** They decide:

✓ Do I want something serious, or just something casual?

✓ Does this woman add value to my life?

✓ Am I setting the right expectations upfront?

The key? Be clear on what you want—before she asks.

If you don't take control of the direction, she will. And **that's when guys end up in the wrong situations.**

The 3 Paths a Connection Can Take

1. Casual Encounter – Purely physical, no emotional attachment.

2. Friends with Benefits – A mix of physical and friendly, but no commitment.

3. Meaningful Relationship – Deeper emotional and physical connection.

Pro Tip: There's no right or wrong—**only what aligns with your lifestyle and goals.**

Now, let's break down how to **set expectations, keep things exciting, and avoid common mistakes.**

If You Want a Casual Encounter

How to Set the Right Expectations:

✓ **Be clear, but smooth.** You don't need to say, "I just want something casual." Instead, communicate it through action.

✓ **Frame it as a mutual experience.** Women respect men who own their intentions—without making it all about them.

✓ **Never mislead her.** If she's looking for commitment and you're not, **be upfront.**

What to Say:

"I like keeping things simple, fun, and in the moment. No pressure, just good times."

"I'm focused on my goals right now, so I'm not looking for anything serious—but I love great connections."

Pro Tip: Women appreciate honesty more than fake promises. If she's not into casual, respect that and move on.

If You Want a Friends with Benefits Situation

How to Make It Work (Without Drama):

✓ **Set boundaries early.** (No unnecessary texting, no meeting the parents, etc.)

✓ **Keep emotions in check.** (Don't act like her boyfriend.)

✓ **Let her feel like it's her choice.** (Women love feeling like they're in control.)

What to Say:

"I like having deep connections without pressure. Let's just enjoy the moment and see where it goes."

"We have great chemistry, and I love spending time together—but I want to keep things light and easy."

Pro Tip: The best way to keep a FWB situation healthy? **Have your own life outside of it.**

If You Want a Meaningful Relationship

A relationship should ADD to your life—not become your life.

How to Make Her Invest in You:

✓ **Make her earn your commitment.** Don't just jump in—see if she's the right fit.

✓ **Set standards for what you want.** (Respect, loyalty, support, chemistry.)

✓ **Take your time.** (Attraction is fast, but true compatibility takes time.)

Signs She's a High-Quality Woman for a Relationship: She **respects your time and effort** (No games, no flakiness).

She **supports your mission** (Encourages your goals, not distracts from them).

She **has her own life** (Not overly needy, brings value to your world).

What to Say:

"I'm looking for something real—but only if it's with the right person."

"I don't rush into relationships—I take my time and see if we're truly aligned."

Pro Tip: The moment you **stop chasing a relationship and start qualifying women for it**, everything changes.

The #1 Mistake That Kills Relationships (Or Casual Situations)

Letting attraction fade.

Women don't stay interested just because they like you at first.

How to Keep the Spark Alive:

✓ **Continue flirting and teasing**—even after you're together.

✓ **Keep your own life exciting**—never revolve your world around her.

✓ **Occasionally pull away and let her miss you.**

Pro Tip: Attraction is **not just about getting the girl—it's about keeping the excitement alive.**

How to Know When to Walk Away

A high-value man doesn't stay in situations that don't serve him.

Red Flags That Show She's Not Right for You:

She's **constantly testing you in unhealthy ways.**

She **disrespects your time, goals, or boundaries.**

She **tries to control you, guilt-trip you, or play games.**

What to Do if She's Becoming Too Much Work:

Pull back. If she values you, she'll correct her behavior.
Call it out. If she's disrespectful, let her know it's

unacceptable.

Walk away if needed. Never be afraid to leave a bad situation.

Pro Tip: The strongest negotiating position in any relationship? **Being willing to walk away.**

The Takeaway

You decide what kind of connection you want—not her.

If you master:

Setting clear expectations (Casual, FWB, or relationship)

Keeping attraction alive (Never get complacent)

Walking away when needed (Confidence is knowing your worth)

…then **you'll never feel like you "lost control" of a situation again.**

Women respect men who know what they want and stand by it.

Chapter 17

The Long-Term Game – Keeping Her Interested and Avoiding Complacency

Why Most Men Lose Women Over Time

Getting the girl is easy—keeping her interested is where most men fail.

Most guys make the mistake of **getting comfortable** and thinking attraction is permanent.

But **women don't fall for a man once—they keep falling for him over time.**

If you stop:
Flirting with her.
Bringing excitement to the relationship.
Growing and improving yourself.

…then **attraction dies, and she will lose interest.**

The key? Keep the energy, attraction, and excitement alive—no matter how long you've been together.

The 3 Rules for Keeping Her Hooked Long-Term

1. Never Stop Being the Man She Was Attracted To.
2. Keep Her Emotionally Engaged and Challenged.
3. Maintain Your Own Mission and Growth.

Let's break each one down.

1. Never Stop Being the Man She Was Attracted To

Most men change after they "get" the girl.

They:
Stop working out.

Stop flirting and teasing.

Become overly available and predictable.

How to Keep Attraction Alive:

✓ Continue **challenging and teasing her.** (Don't become boring.)

✓ Stay **in shape and well-groomed.** (Attraction is visual.)

✓ Keep **being social and desirable.** (Women want men who are valued by others.)

Pro Tip: She was attracted to your **energy, confidence, and ambition**—never let those fade.

2. Keep Her Emotionally Engaged and Challenged

Women need emotional stimulation to stay attracted.

Most men get too predictable and stop:
Creating new experiences.
Keeping a little mystery alive.
Keeping the playful challenge in the relationship.

How to Keep Her Emotionally Hooked:

✓ **Keep surprising her.** (Spontaneous date nights, small thoughtful gestures.)

✓ **Playfully challenge her.** ("I think you're getting too comfortable—time to impress me.")

✓ **Occasionally pull back.** (A little distance makes her miss you.)

Pro Tip: Women don't want perfection—they want **excitement and unpredictability.**

---

3. Maintain Your Own Mission and Growth

Men lose women when they make her the center of their world.

Attraction **dies** when she realizes:
You stopped chasing your dreams.
You prioritize her over your own mission.
You've become **dependent on her for happiness.**

How to Keep Your Value High:

✓ Stay **focused on your goals and passions.**
✓ Keep **building your social and professional life.**
✓ Never **become needy or dependent on her attention.**

Pro Tip: The moment she feels like she's "completed" you, **she will start losing interest.**

The Biggest Mistake That Destroys Long-Term Attraction

Getting complacent.

Most men:
Stop putting in effort.
Assume she will always feel attraction.
Become predictable and routine.

The truth? Women will only stay attracted if you keep giving them reasons to.

Fix it by:

✓ Continuing to **flirt, tease, and keep the energy alive.**
✓ Keeping **a little mystery and independence.**
✓ Always **growing and improving.**

Pro Tip: Attraction is like a fire—if you don't keep adding fuel, it burns out.

How to Keep Her Chasing You in a Long-Term Relationship

The best relationships are when she still feels like she's earning your attention.

How to Make Her Invest in You Over Time:

✓ **Don't always be available.** (Have your own life and purpose.)
✓ **Let her wonder about you occasionally.** (Stay a little unpredictable.)
✓ **Keep your standards high.** (She should always feel like she's with a man of value.)

Pro Tip: The moment she feels like she doesn't have to put in effort, **she'll start losing interest.**

The Takeaway

Attraction isn't a one-time thing—it's something you build and maintain.

If you master:

Staying the high-value man she fell for (Confidence, ambition, energy)

Keeping her emotionally engaged (Surprise, unpredictability, challenge)

Maintaining your own life and mission (Never making her your sole focus)

…then **she will stay attracted, engaged, and excited to be with you—long-term.**

Most men get the girl. High-value men keep her interested.

Chapter 18

Mastering the Breakup – When to Walk Away and How to Move On

Why Walking Away is One of the Most Powerful Skills a Man Can Have

Most men stay in relationships far longer than they should.

They ignore the red flags, settle for **less than they deserve**, and hold onto something **that's already broken.**

Why?

Fear of being alone.

Emotional attachment and nostalgia.

The sunk cost fallacy—staying because of "all the time invested."

But here's the truth:

✓ **Walking away from the wrong relationship makes pace for the right one.**

✓ **A man who knows his worth never begs for love.**

✓ **The ability to leave makes you more attractive—both to her and to yourself.**

Let's break down **when to walk away, how to do it like a high-value man, and how to move on fast.**

When to Walk Away from a Relationship

The biggest mistake men make? Staying in a bad relationship because they "hope things will get better."

Signs It's Time to Leave:

She disrespects you. (Lies, manipulation, lack of appreciation.)
You feel drained instead of energized. (Love should lift you, not exhaust you.)

The attraction and excitement are gone. (You're staying out of habit, not passion.)

She tries to control you. (Jealousy, guilt-tripping, constant demands.)
You've outgrown her. (She no longer aligns with your vision for life.)

Pro Tip: A high-value man doesn't tolerate bad behavior—he walks away the moment he sees it.

How to End a Relationship Like a High-Value Man

Most men either:

Drag out a breakup and suffer for months.

Act needy, trying to "fix" things when it's already over. Get emotional and lose their power.

The Right Way to End It:

✓ **Stay calm and composed.** (No drama, no arguing.)

✓ **Be direct, but not cruel.** ("I don't see this working anymore, and I think it's best we go our separate ways.")

✓ **Cut ties completely.** (No "let's stay friends" or checking up on her.)

✓ **Don't explain yourself endlessly.** (You don't need her approval to leave.)

Golden Rule: The **faster and cleaner the breakup, the easier it is to move on.**

Pro Tip: Women respect men who can **walk away without looking back.**

What to Do If She Tries to Get You Back

Women often want you back when they see you moving on.

If she reaches out after the breakup:

✓ **Ask yourself:** Do I actually want her back, or is this just comfort?

✓ **If she truly changed, she'll show it through actions—not words.**

✓ **If you don't want her back, don't engage.** (No mixed signals.)

Pro Tip: The best revenge? **Leveling up and living better than ever.**

How to Move On Fast (And Come Back Stronger Than Before)

The secret to moving on quickly? Focus forward, not backward.

Step 1: Go No Contact.

✓ **Block or mute her.**

✓ **Don't stalk her social media.**

✓ **Cut off all unnecessary connections.**

Step 2: Hit the Gym & Improve Yourself.

✓ Use that energy to build a better body, mindset, and lifestyle.

✓ The best way to get over someone? Become someone even better.

Step 3: Reconnect with Your Mission.

✓ Your life doesn't revolve around women—build your empire.

✓ Invest in your goals, passions, and purpose.

Step 4: Get Back Out There (When You're Ready).

✓ Don't rush—heal first.

✓ When you're ready, meet new women without expectations.

✓ Date as a high-value man—not as someone looking for validation.

Pro Tip: The fastest way to move on is to become the version of yourself you always wanted to be.

The #1 Mistake That Keeps Men Stuck After a Breakup

Holding onto false hope.

Stop waiting for her to change, regret, or come back.

Instead, focus on:

✓ **Your growth.** (Become stronger than before.)
✓ **Your goals.** (Build your future without her.)
✓ **New experiences.** (Expand your social circle and skills.)

Pro Tip: She's your past. Your future is waiting for you.

The Takeaway

A man who knows his worth never begs for love.

If you master:

Knowing when to walk away. (Recognizing red flags early.)
Ending things cleanly. (No drawn-out drama.)
Moving on with confidence. (Leveling up, not looking back.)

…then **you'll never fear a breakup again.**

Walking away from the wrong person is what makes space for the right one.

Chapter 19

The Mindset of a Man Who Never Struggles with Women

Why Mindset is Everything

The difference between men who succeed with women and those who struggle?

It's **not looks.**
It's **not money.**
It's **not memorized pickup lines.**

It's mindset.

High-value men think **differently** about:

✓ **Themselves** (Confidence comes from within.)
✓ **Women** (They are abundant, not rare.)
✓ **Rejection** (It's just part of the process.)
✓ **Dating** (It's about fun and connection—not proving yourself.)

If you **fix your mindset, you'll never struggle with women again.**

The 5 Core Beliefs of a Man Who Never Struggles with Women

1. "I Am the Prize."
2. "I Don't Chase, I Attract."
3. "Rejection Means Nothing to Me."
4. "I Am Always Improving."
5. "Women Are a Part of My Life—Not My Purpose."

Let's break each one down.

---

1. "I Am the Prize."

Most men put women on a pedestal.

They think:
"I hope she likes me."
"I have to impress her."
"She's out of my league."

High-value men think differently:

✓ "I have value—I'm seeing if she's good enough for me."

✓ "I don't need to prove myself—she needs to prove she deserves my time."

✓ "I bring something unique—if she doesn't see it, that's her loss."

Golden Rule: Women want men they **earn**—not men who beg for their attention.

Pro Tip: Flip the frame—YOU are the prize. The moment you believe this, women will feel it.

---

2. "I Don't Chase, I Attract."

Men who struggle chase women.

High-value men **make women chase them.**

How to Stop Chasing and Start Attracting:
✓ **Live a life so exciting that women want to be part of it.**
✓ **Be selective—only pursue women who show interest.**
✓ **Make her work for you, too.**

Example:
Chasing: "Why haven't you texted me back?"
Attracting: "I don't wait on texts—I'm too busy having fun."

Pro Tip: The moment you stop chasing, women start chasing you.

---

3. "Rejection Means Nothing to Me."

Men who struggle with women fear rejection.

High-value men understand:

✓ **Rejection isn't personal.** (She doesn't even know you—how can she reject you?)

✓ **Rejection is necessary.** (Every "no" brings you closer to a "yes.")

✓ **Rejection is proof you're taking action.**

Example:
Low-value mindset: "I got rejected, I must not be good enough."
High-value mindset: "She wasn't a match—next."

Pro Tip: The less you care about rejection, the more women will be drawn to you.

---

4. "I Am Always Improving."

Most men stop improving once they get comfortable. High-value men keep leveling up—no matter what.

✓ They stay **fit and healthy.**

✓ They grow **mentally, financially, and socially.**

✓ They always **work on their mindset.**

Golden Rule: The better you become, the better women you attract.

Pro Tip: Make self-improvement a lifelong habit, and success with women will follow naturally.

---

5. "Women Are a Part of My Life—Not My Purpose."

Men who struggle make women their goal.

They think:

"If I get a girlfriend, I'll be happy."

"I just need to find the perfect girl."

High-value men think differently:

✓ "Women are a complement to my life—not the center of it."
✓ "My mission comes first—women are a bonus."
✓ "I don't need a woman to be complete—I'm already complete."

Example:

Low-value mindset: "I'll do whatever it takes to keep her."
High-value mindset: "If she adds value, she can stay. If not, I walk."

Pro Tip: When women see you have a purpose beyond them, they respect and desire you more.

The #1 Mindset Shift That Changes Everything

Stop asking, "How can I get women to like me?"

Instead, ask:

✓ "How can I be the best version of myself?"

✓ "How can I create a life so great that women want to be part of it?"

✓ "How can I stop chasing and start attracting?"

Golden Rule: Success with women isn't about THEM—it's about YOU.

Pro Tip: The moment you **shift your focus to becoming a high-value man**, women will start appearing in your life effortlessly.

The Takeaway

If you want to never struggle with women again, change your mindset.

If you master:

Seeing yourself as the prize. (You don't chase—you attract.)
Embracing rejection as part of the game. (It means nothing.)
Focusing on self-improvement. (Better you = better women.)
Putting your mission first. (Women respect men with purpose.)

…then **you'll become the kind of man women naturally want to be around.**

Success with women isn't about tricks—it's about being a man who naturally attracts.

Chapter 20

Final Thoughts – Becoming the Man You Were Meant to Be

This Isn't Just About Women—It's About Becoming Your Best Self

If you've made it this far, you already understand something most men never do:

Success with women isn't about tricks, pickup lines, or playing games.

It's about becoming the most confident, attractive, high-value version of yourself.

When you focus on becoming a powerful man, women naturally become drawn to you.

This journey isn't just about dating—it's about **mastering your life.**

The 7 Principles of a High-Value Man

If you live by these, you'll never struggle—not just with women, but in life.

1. Confidence is Everything.

✓ The way you carry yourself shapes how others treat you.

✓ You don't ask for permission—you take what you want.

✓ You believe in yourself, even when others don't.

2. Rejection is Just Part of the Game.

✓ You don't fear rejection—you embrace it.

✓ Every "no" gets you closer to a "yes."

✓ You never let rejection shake your self-worth.

3. Women Are Abundant, Not Rare.

✓ You don't chase—because you know there are plenty of amazing women.

✓ You treat every interaction as a chance to connect—not as life or death.

✓ You never cling to one woman out of fear of losing her.

4. You Always Improve Yourself.

✓ You stay in great shape, dress well, and take care of yourself.

✓ You keep leveling up—mentally, financially, and socially.

✓ You never settle or stagnate.

5. You Lead Every Interaction.

✓ Women respect and follow a man who leads.

✓ You make decisions with confidence and own your actions.

✓ You never hesitate when it's time to make a move.

6. You Never Let a Woman Control Your Life.

✓ You don't change who you are just to please her.

✓ You don't tolerate disrespect or games.

✓ You put your mission first—always.

7. You Enjoy the Process.

✓ You don't take dating or life too seriously.

✓ You have fun, take risks, and embrace adventure.

✓ You know that being a high-value man is a journey, not a destination.

Pro Tip: If you live by these principles, you won't just attract women—you'll command respect, opportunity, and success in all areas of life.

Your Mission Moving Forward

This book isn't the end—it's the beginning.

Your mission is simple:

✓ **Take action.** (Don't just read—apply what you've learned.)

✓ **Keep growing.** (You're never "done" improving.)

✓ **Live with confidence, purpose, and boldness.**

Remember: Women don't want a perfect man. They want a man who is:

✓ Confident in himself.

✓ Passionate about his mission.

✓ Exciting and unpredictable.

✓ In control of his own life.

You have everything it takes to be that man. Now go out and live it.

The Final Takeaway

You don't need luck, tricks, or gimmicks to succeed with women.

You just need to become the kind of man who naturally attracts.

✓ Confidence.

✓ Purpose.

✓ Social intelligence.

✓ The ability to lead.

If you master these, **everything else will fall into place.**

Pro Tip: Women come and go, but your growth as a man lasts forever.

Go out there and own your life. The world is yours.

Appendix

The 20 Laws of Attraction and Seduction

"Seduction is not a game of words—it is a way of being."

These laws are not just rules. They are a **philosophy—a way of life.**

You will record them, listen to them daily, and embody them.

They will transform you into a man who:
✓ **Attracts without effort.**

✓ **Influences without force.**

✓ **Leaves an unforgettable impact on every woman he meets.**

Law #1: Become the Prize – She Must Earn You

"A king does not beg—he is pursued."

Most men try to prove themselves to women. High-value men **position themselves as the prize.**

Your Daily Commandment:

"I am the prize. I do not chase—I attract."

Law #2: Speak with Your Presence, Not Just Your Words

"True seduction begins before a single word is spoken."

Your **eye contact, body language, and energy** say more than words ever could.

Master **silent confidence**, and women will be drawn to you before you even open your mouth.

Your Daily Commandment:

"My presence speaks louder than my words. I own every space I enter."

Law #3: Keep Her Guessing – Never Be Predictable

"Mystery is the oxygen of desire."

The moment a woman **thinks she has you figured out**, attraction fades.

Stay **unpredictable, elusive, and slightly out of reach.**

Your Daily Commandment:

"I remain a mystery. She must work to unlock me."

Law #4: Flirt Like a Shadow – Be Playful, Yet Unattainable

"Seduction is a dance—tease, retreat, advance."

Give her a taste of your attention, then pull away. Flirting is **push-pull, tension, and unpredictability.**

Your Daily Commandment:

"I create tension. I am playful, yet always in control."

Law #5: Let Silence Build Desire

"**The man who can sit in silence holds all the power.**"

Most men talk too much—trying to fill every gap. Powerful men **let silence create intrigue.**

Your Daily Commandment:

"My silence is my weapon. It makes her lean in."

Law #6: Touch Creates Reality – Escalate Naturally

"**What is unspoken but felt is more powerful than words.**"

A single touch can communicate more than an hour of talking.
Slow, deliberate, and natural touch builds deep attraction.

Your Daily Commandment:

"I use touch to create connection. It is natural, confident, and never forced."

Law #7: Make Her Feel, Not Just Think

"**Attraction is emotional, not logical.**"

Women do not **fall for facts**—**they fall for feelings**. Move her **emotionally**—through energy, adventure, and mystery.

Your Daily Commandment:

"I am the source of excitement and emotion. I make her feel something real."

Law #8: Control the Frame – Never Let Her Lead You

"The man who controls the frame controls the interaction."

If you let her **dictate the energy**, you lose attraction. You set the tone. You decide the pace.

Your Daily Commandment:

"I control the frame. I lead—she follows."

Law #9: Speak Slowly, Move Deliberately

"A man who speaks slowly forces the world to listen."

The slower you talk, the more powerful you seem. Fast movements **signal nervousness**—slow, deliberate movements **signal control**.

Your Daily Commandment:

"I move with certainty. My words and actions command attention."

Law #10: Give Her the Gift of Chasing You

"Desire grows in absence, not in excess."

Give her attention, then withdraw.

Let **her** crave more.

Your Daily Commandment:

"I give sparingly, making my attention valuable."

Law #11: Let Her Earn Your Time and Attention

"Never give freely what must be earned."

Most men seek to **win over women.**

High-value men **let women earn them.**

Your Daily Commandment:

"My time is valuable—she must prove she deserves it."

Law #12: Own the Room Without Trying

"The most powerful presence is the one that does not seek approval."

Do not try to **dominate a room**—own it by simply **existing with confidence.**

Women notice the man who **moves with calm certainty.**

Your Daily Commandment:

"My presence is effortless. People feel my energy without me forcing it."

Law #13: Always Be Willing to Walk Away

"The man who is not afraid to lose always wins."

Women respect men **who do not cling, beg, or compromise their worth.**

The strongest position in any relationship? **Being willing to walk away.**

Your Daily Commandment:

"I am never afraid to walk away. My value is undeniable."

Law #14: Make Her Feel Like She's Special—But Not the Only One

"Every woman wants to feel chosen, but never taken for granted."

Give her **just enough attention** to feel desired—but never **so much that she feels she's already won you.**

Your Daily Commandment:

"I make her feel unique, but I never give myself away completely."

Law #15: Never Give Too Much, Too Soon

"Abundance is created through scarcity."

Men who **give everything too soon** become less valuable. Hold back just enough to **keep her wanting more.**

Your Daily Commandment:

"I give in doses. I let her crave more."

Law #16: Keep Your Mystery Alive

"The man who is fully known is no longer exciting."

Never **reveal everything at once.**

Keep her **guessing, wondering, wanting more.**

Your Daily Commandment:

"I remain a mystery—always intriguing, never fully known."

Law #17: Lead With Adventure, Not Validation

"Women crave men who bring excitement, not compliments."

Most men **validate** women.

High-value men **bring adventure into their lives.**

Your Daily Commandment:

"I am the adventure. I bring excitement, not approval-seeking."

Law #18: Make Her Earn Your Commitment

"A man who commits too easily loses value."

Women do not **respect what is given freely.**

Let her **work for your commitment.**

Your Daily Commandment:

"My commitment is valuable—only the right woman will earn it."

Law #19: Stay Unshaken by Her Tests

"**Women test men to see if they are strong.**"

If you fail the test, attraction **fades instantly.**

Stay **calm, unfazed, and in control.**

Your Daily Commandment:

"I am unshaken. Tests do not affect me—I remain the mountain."

Law #20: Keep Your Mission First

"**Your purpose is your power—never lose sight of it.**"

A man who **revolves his life around a woman loses himself.**

Your **mission comes first. Always.**

Your Daily Commandment:

"My mission is my priority. Women admire, but never define me."

These are the 20 Laws of Attraction and Seduction.

Record them. Listen to them daily. Live them.

The world will bend to your presence. Women will chase you. **And you will never struggle again.**

About the Author

Chase M. Klein is a husband of 18 years, a devoted father of two, and a businessman who has built and led multiple successful sales companies. His career has been shaped by an unwavering commitment to understanding human behavior, influence, and the psychology of persuasion.

Through years of observation, he has come to recognize a fundamental truth that many men either ignore or refuse to confront: 80% of women are choosing to be with only 20% of men. The implications of this are staggering, yet the reasons behind it are rarely examined with intellectual honesty.

Klein contends that seduction is not simply a matter of luck, nor is it a passive phenomenon that occurs randomly. It is, at its core, a learned skill, one that operates under principles similar to those that govern success in business, leadership, and negotiation. Attraction and seduction are not the same thing. Attraction is automatic, a natural response requiring little effort. Seduction, however, is deliberate. It is an active process, one that requires discipline, refinement, and a deep understanding of human nature.

In this book, Klein applies the same rigorous approach that has made him a leader in sales and persuasion to the art of seduction, revealing the strategies that separate the men who struggle from those who thrive. His work is not about deception or manipulation, it is about understanding reality, adapting to it, and mastering the skills that lead to success, both in business and in life.

Made in United States
Orlando, FL
10 May 2025